HOW MUCH
IS THAT WORTH?

by
Lionel Munby

Published by PHILLIMORE for
BRITISH ASSOCIATION FOR LOCAL HISTORY

HOW MUCH IS THAT WORTH?

First published 1989

SECOND EDITION

Published 1996 by Phillimore & Co. Ltd.
Shopwyke Manor Barn CHICHESTER PO20 6BG

for British Association for Local History
24 Lower Street, Harnham SALISBURY SP2 8EY

(General Editor: Alan G. Crosby)

© Lionel M. Munby 1996

Designed and printed by Salisbury Printing Company Ltd.
Greencroft Street SALISBURY SP1 1JF

ISBN 0 85033 741 0

The Banker and his Wife, by Quinten Metsys, 1514. Reproduced by permission of the Musée du Louvre.

CONTENTS

List of tables 8

List of illustrations 9

General Editor's introduction 10

Acknowledgements 11

A note on currency 13

How Much Is That Worth? Why there is no simple answer 17

How indexes are produced 21

Cost-of-living indexes produced and used by 20th-century governments 22

Indexes measuring wages and standards of living 26

Some examples of actual prices paid for particular items 28

Statistical Appendix

PRE-20TH-CENTURY INDEXES

    Medieval to modern 34

        Phelps Brown and Hopkins 34

        Bank of England: equivalent values of the pound 38

    Sixteenth to seventeenth centuries 40

        Phelps Brown and Hopkins 40

        Peter Bowden 41

    Seventeenth to eighteenth centuries 44

        Peter Bowden 44

        Elizabeth Gilboy 46

    The nineteenth century (1780-1914) 49

        N. J. Silberling: Cost of living 49

        Charles Feinstein: Cost of living 50

            Allocation of working-class expenditure on food 50

            New cost of living index 1780-1870 52

            Cost of living index 1870-1914 53

        Charles Feinstein: real earnings 55

TWENTIETH-CENTURY OFFICIAL (GOVERNMENT) INDEXES

    Cost of living 8

        Weighting 9

        Indexes of retail prices 60

        Index and weighting figures 1914-1994 60

        Index of retail prices 1900-1992 62

        Purchasing power of the pound 1900-1993 62

    Wage rates 63

    Earnings 66

LIST OF TABLES

Coins: a summary table 14

Conversion table: coins and notes 14

Decimal currency converter 15

Index of consumables and wage-rates 1264-1954 35-37

Equivalent contemporary values of the pound 1270-1992 38-39

Index of foodstuffs and industrial products 1451-1700 40

Index of agricultural commodities 1450-1649 41

Index of agricultural day wage rates 1450-1649 43

Index of agricultural commodities 1640-1749 44

Index of agricultural day wage rates 1640-1749 45

Cost of living index 1700-1815 46

Wages index 1700-1796 47

Allocation of working class expenditure on food 50

New cost of living index 1780-1870 52

Cost of living index 1870-1914 53-54

Indices of nominal/real earnings and cost of living 1790-1900 56

Weighting in cost of living indexes 59

Indexes of retail prices 1914-1994 60-61

Index of retail prices 1900-1992 62

Purchasing power of the pound 1900-1993 62

Wage rates indexes, 20th century 63-65

Index of earnings 1967-1993 66

LIST OF ILLUSTRATIONS

Food purchased for a large country house in (1637) 19

A contemporary explanation of a sharp fall in prices (1832) 23

Conflicting evidence on prices and the economy (1879) 25

Factory inspector's report on women's wages (1917) 27

Legally-binding wages fixed by magistrates (17th century) 29

Probate inventory of a Carlisle shopkeeper (1571) 31

Shops in the Market Place St. Albans (1897 and 1930) 33

Silver pennies of Edward the Confessor 41

Penny of William I or William II 42

Silver penny of Henry I 43

Silver farthing of Edward III 43

Silver groat of Edward III 45

Silver groat of Edward IV 45

Minting coin in 15th century 48

Mint Press Room at the Tower of London in 18th century 48

Silver halfpennies of Henry VIII issued under Edward VI 49

Silver testoon of Henry VIII 51

Silver groat of Henry VIII issued under Edward VI 51

Silver shilling of Elizabeth I 51

Silver halfpennies of Elizabeth I 55

Silver crown of William III and Mary II 55

Silver Maundy coins of William III and Mary II 55

Terms of payment for work by Capability Brown at Sherborne Castle 57

A room at Bank of England in about 1695 57

Copper halfpenny of George I 59

Copper halfpenny of George II 59

Copper penny of George III 61

Copper 'cartwheel' twopence of George III 64

Difficulties in calculating real earnings (1913) 65

GENERAL EDITOR'S INTRODUCTION

Whenever one encounters references, in a historical document or printed source, to sums of money in previous centuries questions arise. Even if only subconsciously we make arbitrary conversions to what we think, or hope, are contemporary equivalents: 'multiply by a thousand ... let's say 250 times ... well, £5 a week was a good wage even in 1938'. Most historians encounter such situations regularly, but our knowledge of the real changes in monetary values and purchasing power is likely to be scanty, so our questions remain unanswered or we resort to random guesswork.

See-saw, Margery Daw
Johnny shall have a new master
He shall have but a penny a day
Because he can't work any faster

If poor Johnny was working today, what would that penny mean in contemporary terms? How worthwhile were the countless small sums given out in poor relief? How valuable were the sums paid for goods recorded in household accounts?

It is rarely possible to answer such questions with absolute confidence. Not only has the value of money changed, but the nature and operation of the mechanisms of the economy have altered beyond recognition. Nonetheless, the importance of these questions remains, and the social and economic relevance of trends in earnings and prices, the need to be able to compare between periods and between different places or regions, and the ever-present interest in that basic question, 'What was that worth', mean that a handbook on the subject is an essential tool for many local and family historians.

In 1989 Lionel Munby, one of our most experienced local historians, published *How Much Is That Worth?* for the British Association of Local History, the first time that such an accessible and comprehensible reference work was available. The book, a best-seller from the day of publication, was a distillation of the material contained in numerous tables and densely-argued articles in journals and textbooks of economic history and statistics.

For this, the 2nd edition, the author has completely revised the text, bringing it fully up-to-date by adding recent economic figures and by including the fruits of the latest researches, conducted in the late 1980s and early 1990s. The result is almost a new book – one which will continue to be of great value to local and family historians and which will remain the only user-friendly work on the subject.

ALAN CROSBY

ACKNOWLEDGEMENTS TO FIRST EDITION

I owe a great deal to advice and suggestions from many people: John Burnett, Christopher Challis, Patricia Knowlden, David Palliser, Bill Serjeant, Kate Tiller, John Whyman, Edward Martin of the Suffolk Archaeological Unit (who provided captions for the drawings of coins) and, above all, David Dymond, B.A.L.H.'s General Editor. Without such help this publication would be even more inadequate, less able to meet the needs of a beginner, than it is. For its surviving insufficiencies I must take full responsibility.

In the second part, the Statistical Appendix, tables from a great variety of sources have been reproduced. In every case the source has been indicated and readers should appreciate that for a full understanding the original article or book must be consulted. An introductory study like this would have been inconceivable without the pioneering researches of several generations of scholars who have produced the indexes used in this publication. In almost all relevant cases 1986 is the most recent year for which information can be found; it has, therefore, been used as the standard year for comparisons.

In 1971 the standard British coinage was changed to a decimal system. A *Note on Currency*, explaining this and earlier coinage, follows. The symbols of the pre-decimal coinage (£.s.d.) are used in the text.

L. M. M. 1988

ACKNOWLEDGEMENTS TO SECOND EDITION

I have used this second edition to bring up to date the tables in the Statistical Appendix and relevant passages in the introductory essay. In one or two places I have altered the text to make the sense clearer. The introductory explanations to many of the tables have been enlarged at the suggestion of BALH's present General Editor, Alan Crosby, without whom this new edition would not be appearing. I have completely redrafted the two sections covering the years 1780-1914 combining them and using the invaluable new research of Prof. Charles Feinstein, to whom I am deeply indebted.

Several other new tables are included. I am grateful to the librarian of the Marshall Library, University of Cambridge for guiding me through the statistical sources which I have used.

L. M. M. 1995

A NOTE ON CURRENCY

In 1971 the old British currency of pounds (£), shillings (s.) and pence (d.) was abandoned for a decimal currency of pounds (£) and new pence (p.). The conversion table below will enable readers to interpret the units of currency mentioned in the text. There were many coins in use before 1971 which became obsolete long before that date. Some are illustrated in this booklet.

Until the late 13th century the only coin actually minted was the **penny**, made of silver; 240 of these silver coins weighed one pound (lb). There developed 'money of account', that is units in which money sums were calculated but which were not produced as coins. The **pound** (240 pennies) and the **shilling** (12 pennies) began like this. The **mark**, **half** and **quarter marks** were commonly used units of money of account. A mark was 160 pennies, that is 13s. 4d., or two-thirds of a pound.

From the 14th century new coins, representing units of money used in accounting, were minted: the **farthing**, a quarter of a penny, from 1279; the **halfpenny** from 1280. Before these new round coins were minted, the silver penny had been physically cut in half and into quarters. The farthing ceased to be legal currency in 1961, the halfpenny in 1969. A new coin, the **groat**, worth four pennies (4d.) was first issued and immediately withdrawn in 1279, but reissued in 1351, along with a **half-groat** (2d.). **Florins**, gold coins, were issued in 1344 but replaced immediately by the **noble** (6s.8d.), with **half** and **quarter nobles**. In 1465 the noble was replaced by the **angel**, which was minted until the 17th century, and by the **royal** or **rose noble** which did not last so long.

A **pound sovereign**, a large gold coin worth 240 pennies or 20 shillings (20s.) was first minted by Henry VII in 1489. In Edward VI's and Mary I's reigns it was revalued at 30 shillings. Elizabeth I minted a 30s. gold **sovereign** and a 20s. gold **pound**. In 1604 James I replaced the pound coin with a **unite** which lasted until 1663 when the **guinea** replaced it. In 1717 the guinea was revalued at 21s. and was last coined in 1813. A standard gold sovereign (20s.) replaced it in 1817 and was minted until 1925. The shilling (12d.), of silver, was first minted by Henry VII after 1504. The **crown** (5s.) and the **half-crown** appeared in 1526. The crown became restricted to special issues only. half-crowns were withdrawn in 1969. A copper penny was minted in 1797, bronze pennies from 1860. The medieval **florin** was revived in 1849 as a 2s. piece.

Coins: a summary table

FARTHING	¼d.			Quarter-Noble	1s.8d.	=	20d.
HALFPENNY	½d.			FLORIN	2s.	=	24d.
PENNY	1d.			HALF-CROWN	2s.6d.	=	30d.
Half-groat	2d.			Half-Noble	3s.4d.	=	40d.
THREEPENCE	3d.			Crown	5s.	=	60d.
Groat	4d.			Noble, Angel, Royal	6s.8d.	=	80d.
SIXPENCE	6d.			Pound, Unite	20s.	=	240d.
SHILLING	1s.	=	12d.	Guinea (from 1717)	21s.	=	252d.

Coins listed in CAPITALS were in regular circulation for everyday use until the late 1950s. The halfpenny, penny, threepence, sixpence, shilling and florin survived until the decimalisation of the currency in 1971. Paper notes valued at 10s., £1, £5 and upwards were also used.

Conversion table: coins and paper notes

Decimal currency (after 1971) COIN			Currency before 15 February 1971 COIN	
			¼d.	farthing
			½d.	halfpenny
			1d.	penny
½p	half [new] penny (obsolete)			
1p	[new] penny			
			3d.	three pence
2p	two [new] pence			
			6d.	sixpence
5p	five [new] pence	=	1s.	one shilling
10p	ten [new] pence	=	2s.	florin/two shillings
			2s.6d.	half-crown
20p	twenty [new] pence			
			5s.	crown
50p	fifty [new] pence	=	10s.	ten shillings [note]
£1	one pound	=	£1	one pound [note]

100p = one pound £1 = 20s. (shillings) = 240d. (pence)

Decimal currency converter

Old	New	Old	New	Old	New	Old	New	Old	New	Old	New	Old	New	Old	New	Old	New	Old	New
		2/0	10	4/0	20	6/0	30	8/0	40	10/0	50	12/0	60	14/0	70	16/0	80	18/0	90
1d.	$\frac{1}{2}$	2/1	$10\frac{1}{2}$	4/1	$20\frac{1}{2}$	6/1	$30\frac{1}{2}$	8/1	$40\frac{1}{2}$	10/1	$50\frac{1}{2}$	12/1	$60\frac{1}{2}$	14/1	$70\frac{1}{2}$	16/1	$80\frac{1}{2}$	18/1	$90\frac{1}{2}$
2d.	1	2/2	11	4/2	21	6/2	31	8/2	41	10/2	51	12/2	61	14/2	71	16/2	81	18/2	91
3d.	1	2/3	11	4/3	21	6/3	31	8/3	41	10/3	51	12/3	61	14/3	71	16/3	81	18/3	91
4d.	$1\frac{1}{2}$	2/4	$11\frac{1}{2}$	4/4	$21\frac{1}{2}$	6/4	$31\frac{1}{2}$	8/4	$41\frac{1}{2}$	10/4	$51\frac{1}{2}$	12/4	$61\frac{1}{2}$	14/4	$71\frac{1}{2}$	16/4	$81\frac{1}{2}$	18/4	$1\frac{1}{2}$
5d.	2	2/5	12	4/5	22	6/5	32	8/5	42	10/5	52	12/5	62	14/5	72	16/5	82	18/5	92
6d.	$2\frac{1}{2}$	2/6	$12\frac{1}{2}$	4/6	$22\frac{1}{2}$	6/6	$32\frac{1}{2}$	8/6	$42\frac{1}{2}$	10/6	$52\frac{1}{2}$	12/6	$62\frac{1}{2}$	14/6	$72\frac{1}{2}$	16/6	$82\frac{1}{2}$	18/6	$2\frac{1}{2}$
7d.	3	2/7	13	4/7	23	6/7	33	8/7	43	10/7	53	12/7	63	14/7	73	16/7	83	18/7	93
8d.	$3\frac{1}{2}$	2/8	$13\frac{1}{2}$	4/8	$23\frac{1}{2}$	6/8	$33\frac{1}{2}$	8/8	$43\frac{1}{2}$	10/8	$53\frac{1}{2}$	12/8	$63\frac{1}{2}$	14/8	$73\frac{1}{2}$	16/8	$83\frac{1}{2}$	18/8	$3\frac{1}{2}$
9d.	4	2/9	14	4/9	24	6/9	34	8/9	44	10/9	54	12/9	64	14/9	74	16/9	84	18/9	94
10d.	4	2/10	14	4/10	24	6/10	34	8/10	44	10/10	54	12/10	64	14/10	74	16/10	84	18/10	92
11d.	$4\frac{1}{2}$	2/11	$14\frac{1}{2}$	4/11	$24\frac{1}{2}$	6/11	$34\frac{1}{2}$	8/11	$44\frac{1}{2}$	10/11	$54\frac{1}{2}$	12/11	$64\frac{1}{2}$	14/11	$74\frac{1}{2}$	16/11	$84\frac{1}{2}$	18/11	$94\frac{1}{2}$
1/0	5	3/0	15	5/0	25	7/0	35	9/0	45	11/0	55	13/0	65	15/0	75	17/0	85	19/0	95
1/1	$5\frac{1}{2}$	3/1	$15\frac{1}{2}$	5/1	$25\frac{1}{2}$	7/1	$35\frac{1}{2}$	9/1	$45\frac{1}{2}$	11/1	$55\frac{1}{2}$	13/1	$65\frac{1}{2}$	15/1	$75\frac{1}{2}$	17/1	$85\frac{1}{2}$	19/1	$95\frac{1}{2}$
1/2	6	3/2	16	5/2	26	7/2	36	9/2	46	11/2	56	13/2	66	15/2	76	17/2	86	19/2	96
1/3	6	3/3	16	5/3	26	7/3	36	9/3	46	11/3	56	13/3	66	15/3	76	17/3	86	19/3	96
1/4	$6\frac{1}{2}$	3/4	$16\frac{1}{2}$	5/4	$26\frac{1}{2}$	7/4	$36\frac{1}{2}$	9/4	$46\frac{1}{2}$	11/4	$56\frac{1}{2}$	13/4	$66\frac{1}{2}$	15/4	$76\frac{1}{2}$	17/4	$86\frac{1}{2}$	19/4	$96\frac{1}{2}$
1/5	7	3/5	17	5/5	27	7/5	37	9/5	47	11/5	57	13/5	67	15/5	77	17/5	87	19/5	97
1/6	$7\frac{1}{2}$	3/6	$17\frac{1}{2}$	5/6	$27\frac{1}{2}$	7/6	$37\frac{1}{2}$	9/6	$47\frac{1}{2}$	11/6	$57\frac{1}{2}$	13/6	$67\frac{1}{2}$	15/6	$77\frac{1}{2}$	17/6	$87\frac{1}{2}$	19/6	$97\frac{1}{2}$
1/7	8	3/7	18	5/7	28	7/7	38	9/7	48	11/7	58	13/7	68	15/7	78	17/7	88	19/7	98
1/8	$8\frac{1}{2}$	3/8	$18\frac{1}{2}$	5/8	$28\frac{1}{2}$	7/8	$38\frac{1}{2}$	9/8	$48\frac{1}{2}$	11/8	$58\frac{1}{2}$	13/8	$68\frac{1}{2}$	15/8	$78\frac{1}{2}$	17/8	$88\frac{1}{2}$	19/8	$98\frac{1}{2}$
1/9	9	3/9	19	5/9	29	7/9	39	9/9	49	11/9	59	13/9	69	15/9	79	17/9	89	19/9	99
1/10	9	3/10	19	15/10	29	7/10	39	9/10	49	11/10	59	13/10	69	15/10	79	17/10	89	19/10	99
1/11	$9\frac{1}{2}$	3/11	$19\frac{1}{2}$	5/11	$29\frac{1}{2}$	7/11	$39\frac{1}{2}$	9/11	$49\frac{1}{2}$	11/11	$59\frac{1}{2}$	13/11	$69\frac{1}{2}$	15/11	$79\frac{1}{2}$	17/11	$89\frac{1}{2}$	19/11	$99\frac{1}{2}$

[O. Newman and A. Foster *The Value of a Pound: prices and incomes in Britain 1900-1993*. Gale Research International Ltd. 1995. Appendix, p 306]

HOW MUCH IS THAT WORTH?

INTRODUCTION

Anyone who reads a document or a history book and comes across a sum of money paid in the past is likely to ask, 'How much is that worth today?'. The real value of money is what it will buy. Therefore we have a second and parallel question to answer: how much money was there available to spend? The two are inseparable, for what lies behind our curiosity about the value of money in the past is a desire to find out how people lived. The standard of living at a given time of a given individual, or group of people, depends on how much money can be spent as well as on what it will buy. Neither of these changes, in what money will buy and in money incomes, can be measured simply or exactly. On the few occasions when historians have, almost in throw-away asides, made statements as to overall changes in the value of money, their sums have been very approximate and limited in application. For example Geoffrey Baskerville in his *English Monks and the Suppression of the Monasteries* (1937) 'reckoned the value of money in 1536 to have been about thirty times the present value'.[1] Dr. Hoskins in *The Age of Plunder* (1976) suggested that the £7,000 asked in 1538 for Fountains Abbey and some of its land 'would represent about £750,000 today', that is about a hundred and seven times as much.[2] Either of these two statements would have had meaning when they were first published, but since we live in a period of rapid inflation they become misleading to later readers. During the period between 1937 and 1976, prices rose by over eight times. This means that Baskerville's 1936 estimate of thirty should have been 240 times in 1976, but Hoskins' was only 107. The difference is NOT because these two historians were simply guessing, but because they were dealing with large increases over long periods of time and because they were probably measuring different things. When smallish differences are multiplied by large numbers, as happens when price changes over long periods are calculated, the margins of error become larger. In any case Hoskins was, presumably, measuring changes in property and land values. Baskerville used information provided by Dr. Salter whose calculation of 'between thirty and thirty-five times' was based on incomes and the cost of a meal.[1] As we will see, changes in prices over time might be quite different for different things.

No single, precise, numerical answer is possible to the question: what is the modern value of a given sum of money at a particular time in the past? We do know the monetary price of many distinct items at specific times, but we cannot easily generalise from these prices.

Why there is no simple answer

The chief reasons why no simple answer can be given to the question 'how much is that worth today?' are suggested by the following example. Since money only has value in terms of what it can buy, the modern reader cannot make sense of the one shilling (1s.) left to the poor in a widow's will of 1592 without much more information. When it is explained that the justices of the peace fixed 7d. or 8d. a day as the casual labourer's wage, in the same period, a comparison seems to be possible. The widow was leaving under two days' wages. If we discover what a labourer earned in 1995 we might have a rough modern approximation to what the widow left to the poor. In 1995 the ordinary rate for an agricultural labourer was £149.44 for a 39 hour week, which implies £25 a day. This means that the modern equivalent of the widow's bequest would be £37 (12d: 8d = £37: £25). But this is only one way to measure the 1995 equivalent of the 1592 shilling. A small bequest in the 1590s would probably have been spent on bread; so another way to measure the value of the 1s. would be to find out how much bread could be bought in 1592 for 1s. and what the same amount of bread would cost in 1995. The results of those two comparisons would be quite different. There are further complexities: what kind of bread are we thinking of? Mancheat, the finest wheaten bread, was dearer than bread made of maslin, a mixture of wheat and rye, which was the poor man's bread. In any case it is unlikely that money left to the poor in 1995 would be spent primarily on bread.

The problems which arise in trying to compare what money was worth at different periods in time can be summarised as follows:

1. Are items which *seem* to be the same really so? Can a Tudor loaf of bread, or suit of clothes, or the bricks used in Tudor buildings, be compared precisely with their apparent modern equivalents?

2. Money wages and personal incomes have altered quite differently for different people. In 1995 the Master of the Rolls was paid £109,435. His predecessor in 1636 seems to have made between £1,600 and £2,200 a year. So the money earned by the Master of the Rolls was some fifty to seventy times greater in 1995 than it had been 360 years earlier. By contrast, an agricultural labourer in 1995, with £25 a day, earned some six hundred times the money his predecessor earned in 1636, which was 10d. a day. The immediate simple assumption would therefore be that the gap between the lawyer's and the labourer's standard of living had altered radically in the labourer's favour. This may be true but it does not follow automatically from the changes in the money they received. We need to know what they spent their money on, and how the cost of what they bought has changed.

3. Since the prices paid for different items have not changed in the same way over time, apparent differences in changes in income *may* not represent similar changes in standards of living. In an extreme case, if the price of what the labourer bought had increased some ten times more than the price of what the lawyer bought, there would have been little change in their relative economic positions.

4. Neither prices nor wages have been the same in all parts of the country. In the late 18th century the north-country labourer earned less than his southern counterpart, but lived better because he ate differently and his food was cheaper. A diet of oats, potatoes and milk contrasted with one of wheaten bread and cheese (*see* pp.31-2). When communications were more primitive than they are today this was not surprising, but regional differences in prices are still considerable as anyone knows who has moved house between the north and south. Between 1986 and 1987 an average pay rise of 16.5 per cent was needed to maintain the standard of living of people in Greater London, while in much of northern and midland England this could be achieved on slightly *reduced* pay. Shop prices in Lerwick were 13 per cent higher, in Billingham and Cleveland seven per cent lower, than the national average.

    Money is not, and has not been in the past, worth the same everywhere in Britain. In 1993 total personal income per head averaged £11,982 in London, £10,683 in the rest of the South-East, but only £8,850 in the North and £8,655 in Wales. Consumers' expenditure in the same year varied in the same way: £8,855 in London, £7,731 in the rest of the South-East, but only £6,303 in the North and £6,286 in Wales.[3]

5. We face a further complication: with a rising standard of living and progress in technology there have been major changes in consumer habits. For most periods before the late 19th century, the labourer spent a major portion of his earnings on bread grains. So changes in the price of grain compared with changes in the

Food purchased for a large country house in 1637 — variety, quantity, prices. From The House Book of Gorhambury, Michaelmas 1637 to Michaelmas 1639, in the Hertfordshire Record Office (66,301), and published in *Early Stuart Household Accounts*, ed. L. M. Munby, Hertfordshire Record Soc. (1986), pp. 79-80. Original reproduced by permission of Peter Walne, the former County Archivist.

labourer's earnings can provide a rough indication of whether the labourer was better or worse off in most periods until about a century ago, but not since. It was said in 1899 that the sort of man who had had bread and cheese for dinner forty years ago now demanded a chop. Sir John Clapham, writing of changes between 1881 and 1891, claimed that the labourer's condition 'had greatly improved [for he] eats more butchers' meat'; Clapham went on to point out the limitations of 'a bread calculation' of 'the purchasing power of agricultural day wages'.[4]

In the late 20th century, no grain price is of much importance in measuring the labourer's standard of living. The labourer today not only spends more money on many other foods than grain, but he also spends a much smaller proportion of his earnings on food; he will be paying for furniture and electrical goods not dreamt of by his predecessors. Similarly the successful lawyer three hundred years ago probably spent much more on bricks and mortar and on servants than his modern equivalent.

What all this amounts to is that it is simply not possible to provide a number by which one can multiply a particular sum of money at some past date to turn it into a precise modern equivalent. There would need to be an almost infinite quantity of such 'multipliers': one for oats in the north, another for wheat in the south, one for the moleskin trousers of the labourer, another for the silk shirt of the nobleman, one for bricks, another for stone, and so on. There would be different multipliers for the wages of a Dorset agricultural labourer or a Yorkshire weaver, and for the earnings of a shopkeeper or a doctor. The Bank of England's equivalent values of the pound (pp. 37-38) are inevitably no more than statistical abstractions.

To overcome this difficulty, *as far as is possible*, economists and economic historians have developed cost-of-living indexes to calculate changes in the value of money, and indexes of wage rates and earnings to calculate changes in the amount of money available to different social groups. We all know that money is likely to buy less this year than it did last year. This change is called inflation. Deflation is the opposite. When money buys more this year than it did last year, this change has occurred! Indexes help governments to measure how much inflation or deflation there has been from year to year. Historians can use them to measure changes in the distant past. These indexes make it possible to produce statements about the value of things in the past which have a *general* significance, but when applied to a particular sum of money at a particular time they may be misleading. They are, however, the only tool which we have.

Before explaining what indexes are, how they are produced, and how they may be used, their limitations need to be considered. A cynical expert explaining statistics to the layman in a book written over a third of a century ago complained: 'index numbers are a widespread disease of modern life ... a symptom of the modern disease of constantly trying to keep a close check on everything ... It is scarcely possible to be respectable nowadays unless one owns at least one index number. It is [questionable] whether we would be any the worse off if the whole bag of tricks were scrapped. So many of these index numbers are so ancient and so out of date, so out of touch with reality'. He then went on, more helpfully, to describe index numbers as 'really nothing more than a special kind of average'.[5] This means that when using indexes you have a reasonable, but only approximate, answer to changes in the prices of most objects, though in *some* cases the change may differ considerably from that implied in the index. While the nearest approximation to the truth which we can get may be that prices were rising fast in the last 10 years of the 18th century, from about one third of their level in 1700 to twice that level, index figures will show a 33 per cent increase in 1790, a 79 per cent increase in 1795 with over 100 per cent in 1800 and 1801. Such numbers give a false impression of precision.

Why then have index numbers been used so widely in this book? Simply because we have no other way to give an answer to the question 'How much is that worth?'. Of course there are many records of the prices paid for particular objects at specific times in particular places. Examples are given on pp. 28-32. The problem is, as these examples show, that such evidence is restricted. To give us an effective answer we need the prices paid for every object over a long period of time. Such prices have been collected in two major works, both lengthy — one consisting of seven volumes — and both unlikely to be available except in major libraries.[6] Even these specialist studies can only provide information for the changing prices of a limited range of objects. To help the ordinary interested person studying local or family history, and the student at school or college, to get some idea of changes in the value of money over time from a simpler and accessible source, we must make the best possible use of the indexes which we have, limited though their applications may sometimes be. The deficiencies of each index have to be appreciated, which means explaining how it is calculated.

How indexes are produced

Indexes for earnings are produced by assembling what seem to be normal wage rates and/or earnings for different categories of people and from different parts of the country over a period of time. A 'base' year is chosen, the year against which changes are to be measured. In this base year the different money figures are averaged, and the final figure for the base year is assumed to equal one hundred. The 'averaging' is done by calculating how many people earn each different wage and 'weighting' each money sum in the following way. Supposing Northumberland labourers earned 6s. a week and there were 500 of them, Yorkshire labourers earned 7s. a week and there were 1,000 of them, Buckinghamshire labourers earned 9s. a week and there were 1,000 of them, while Middlesex labourers earned 10s. a week and there were 500 of them, the averaging, 'weighting', would be done by the following sum:

$$
\begin{array}{ccccc}
6s. & x & 500 & = & 3,000s. \\
7s. & x & 1000 & = & 7,000s. \\
9s. & x & 1000 & = & 9,000s. \\
10s. & x & 500 & = & 5,000s.
\end{array}
$$

TOTAL OF LABOURERS   =   3000   24,000s. = TOTAL OF EARNINGS

24,000s (earnings) ÷ 3,000 (labourers) = 8s. average wage.

Therefore 8s. becomes the average wage in the base year.[7]

Figures for later years are calculated in the same way and then turned into percentages of the base-year figure. So if the weekly wage in the base year is 8s. and in a later year 10s., the index is said to have risen from 100 to 125 (8=100 therefore 10=125).

A cost-of-living index is produced in a similar way, by collecting the prices, at particular moments, of what are believed to be common items of consumption. The total spent over a set period by an 'average' individual or family is assumed to equal 100 in the year for which the calculation is first made, the 'base year'. Changes in the value of money, what can be bought for a given sum of money in later years, are calculated by measuring the cost of buying *the same amounts of the same items* as were bought in the base year, totalling this, and then turning the total into a percentage of the base-year total. For example if a family budget in the base year cost £5, and £5.50 in the next year, the cost-of-living index would be said to have risen by 10 per cent, to have become one hundred and ten.

Perhaps the most difficult part of index making for the non-mathematical reader to understand is 'weighting'. This is how it was described in 1944 by the Ministry of Labour in *The Cost of Living Index Number*, using the example of food:

> The average percentage change in the price of each separate article of food having thus been computed, these percentages are then combined so as to obtain a single figure representing the general average increase in food prices since July, 1914 (*see* p. 55-56). The individual percentages vary considerably, milk, for example, having increased in price at 1st June, 1944, by 154 per cent and bread by 55 per cent, on average. As very different proportions of income are spent on milk, bread and other items, it would not be correct simply to add together the percentages shown for these items and divide by the number of items. It is necessary to allow for the difference in the importance of each item in the 1914 budget, and this is done by multiplying each percentage by a number (generally described, for convenience, as a 'weight') based on the relative importance of the several articles and dividing the sum of the products by the sum of these 'weights'. The 'weights' used are as follows: beef 48, mutton 24, bacon 19, fish 9, flour 20, bread 50, tea 22, sugar 19, milk 25, butter 41, cheese 10, margarine 10, eggs 19, potatoes 18, making a total of 334.[8]

Many indexes have been compiled covering prices and wages from the Middle Ages until today. Some of the main ones are printed in the second section of this book, the Statistical Appendix (pp. 33-63). The further back in time, the more limited is the available information. This is even more true of earnings than of prices of goods. Since the number of people in particular occupations or regions is almost unknown in earlier times, so indexes are limited to specific groups of people or particular areas; for example, building craftsmen in the very earliest index, London and Lancashire wages in an index of the 18th-century.

As for cost-of-living indexes, the first question to ask concerns the composition of the packet of prices chosen in the base year. How is it made up? Whose actual expenditure is it supposed to represent? The earlier the period covered, the less likely are we to have reliable information either as to how any large number of people spent their money, or as to what they paid for what they bought. Even the sophisticated indexes developed in the 20th century, which will be discussed in the next section, are far from perfect in these respects.

Cost-of-living indexes produced and used by 20th-century governments

The first official cost-of-living index was introduced in 1914. Ever since then, increasingly highly developed indexes have been produced for both the cost of living and retail prices. These indexes have been, and are, widely used by governments, employers, trade unions, and other social organisations. The brief periods of time for which some of these indexes have been in operation, the frequent changes in weighting, and the great sophistication of the current index, introduced in 1975 (*see* pp. 55-59), should bring home just how impossible it is to calculate *exactly* general changes in the value of money over long periods of time. Any conclusions drawn from the historical indexes already discussed, and printed in the Statistical Appendix on pp. 33-63, *must* therefore be very tentative.

The first government index was already out of date when it was introduced in 1914. A rise or fall only revealed what it was costing, in a given year, to live at the working-class standards of 1904. Even the poorest families in the 1920s and 1930s were not living at the 1904 standard; whether they were worse off or not, they were living differently. 'The cost-of-living index (for example) took account of the cost of paraffin and candles for lighting purposes, and assumed that no working-class family had heard of electricity'![9]

DESCRIPTION.		1818.	1824.	1828.	1830.
	℔	s. d.	s. d.	s. d.	s. d.
Anvils	cwt.	25 0	20 0	16 0	13 0
Awls, polished, Liverpool	gross	2 6	2 0	1 6	1 2
Bed-screws, 6 inches long	gross	18 0	15 0	6 0	5 0
Bits, tinned, for bridles .	doz.	5 0	5 0	3 3	2 6
Bolts for doors, 6 inches	doz.	6 0	5 0	2 3	1 6
Braces for carpenters, with 12 bits	set	9 0	4 0	4 2	3 5
Buttons, for coats	gross	4 6	6 3	3 0	2 2
Buttons, small, for waist-coats, &c.	gross	2 6	2 0	1 2	0 8
Candlesticks, 6 in., brass	pair	2 11	2 0	1 7	1 2
Curry-combs, six barred	doz.	2 9	2 6	1 5	0 11
Frying-pans	cwt.	25 0	21 0	18 0	16 0
Gun-locks, single roller	each	6 0	5 2	1 10	1 6
Hammers, shoe, No. 0 .	doz.	6 9	3 9	3 0	2 9
Hinges, cast-butts, 1 inch	doz.	0 10	0 7½	0 3¾	0 2¾
Knobs, brass, 2 inches for commodes	doz.	4 0	3 6	1 6	1 2
Latches for doors, bright thumb	doz.	2 3	2 2	1 0	0 9
Locks for doors, iron rim, 6 inches	doz.	38 0	32 0	15 0	13 6
Sad-irons & other castings	cwt.	22 6	20 0	14 0	11 6
Shovel & tongs, fire-irons....	pair	1 0	1 0	0 9	0 6
Spoons, tinned table	gross	17 6	15 0	10 0	7 0
Stirrups, plated	pair	4 6	3 9	1 6	1 1
Trace-chains	cwt.	28 0	25 0	19 6	16 6
Trays, japanned tea, 30 inches	each	4 6	3 0	2 0	1 5
Vices for blacksmiths, &c.	cwt.	30 0	28 0	22 0	19 6
Wire, brass	lb.	1 10	1 4	1 0	0 9
—, iron, No. 6	bund	16 0	13 0	9 0	7 0

Prices of the following Articles at Birmingham, in the undermentioned Years.

(204.) The great diminution in price of the articles here enumerated may have arisen from several causes: 1. *The alteration in the value of the currency.* 2. *The increased value of gold in consequence of the increased demand for coin.* The first of these causes may have had some influence ; and the second may have had a very small effect upon the two first quotations of prices, but none at all upon the two latter ones. 3. *The diminished rate of profit produced by capital however employed.* This may be estimated by the average price of three per cents. at the periods stated. 4. *The diminished price of the raw materials out of which these articles were manufactured.* The raw material is principally brass and iron, and the reduction upon it may, in some measure, be estimated by the diminished price of iron and brass wire, in the cost of which articles, the labour bears a less proportion than it does in many of the others. 5. *The smaller quantity of raw material employed, and perhaps, in some instances, an inferior quality of workmanship.* 6. *The improved means by which the same effect was produced by diminished labour.*

A contemporary explanation of a sharp fall in prices. From *On the Economy of Machinery and Manufactures* (1832) by Charles Babbage, Lucasian Professor at Cambridge, pp. 153, 156-7. Babbage was the inventor of a calculating engine, forerunner of the computer.

By 1937 the index had become so blatantly out of date that the Ministry of Labour collected a new sample of working-class family budgets and was about to produce a new index with a new base year, when the Second World War came. The new index was not ready and it proved politically convenient for the government to continue using the 1904/14 index, as an effective means of reducing wartime wage and salary claims based on rises in the cost of living. Rises in wages were based on changes in the index and so kept well below the rise in the real cost of living. What the government did was simple: goods specially prominent in the old cost-of-living index were heavily subsidised by the Treasury and their prices held down in relation to other goods that entered into the expenditure of wage-earners. Some of those subsidised goods were in the paraffin and candles category; others, like eggs, were rationed, so that their actual consumption was compulsorily kept below their weighting. Over half the food items in the 1904 index were subsidised in the Second World War. Because such foods were rationed people spent a much higher proportion of their money on dearer, unsubsidised items than the index allowed for. The price of these unrationed consumption goods was allowed to rise. This wartime policy was described in May 1948 as having

> partially discredited official index numbers in the public's mind. This may eventually prove an expensive price for exploiting public confidence in the cost-of-living index, by selecting items with high weights in the index for subsidising, so as to avoid the necessity for a more rigorous price stabilisation policy.[10]

The resultant cynicism was expressed, bitingly, by a leading statistician in 1951:

> The best known index number is the Cost-of-Living Index, [which is] a rough measure of the basic necessities of life... All we have to do is to invent a 'standard family' (composed of one underpaid male, one overworked female, and 2.2 underfed children) ... We then do a sample survey, to find out what

quantities of the various articles we are considering they consume in a week under normal conditions ... Now it is a relatively simple matter to keep track of the changes in prices as time goes on. It would be very much more troublesome to keep a check on whether the spending pattern, as indicated by the various items bought ... was tending to change; [so we] assume that our standard family will not change its demands from year to year ... our standard family is a standardized family. Its wants are not supposed to change. It is supposed to be devoid of ambition.[11]

Only in 1962, and more completely in 1975, did the official 'Index of Retail Prices' take this criticism into account (see p. 55).

Moroney's irony may serve to underline the difference between numbers and human beings which some historical writers tend to neglect. Statistics deal with abstracts, historians with people who are not abstracts. The statistics do illustrate Moroney's last comments. In the family budgets of 1904, 60 per cent of expenditure was on food, 16 per cent on rent and rates, 12 per cent on clothing, eight per cent on fuel and light, and four per cent was miscellaneous spending. These percentages became the *weights* used each year as long as this index was in use. The budgets collected in 1937-8 revealed a very different pattern of expenditure; this was further modified in an Interim Index of Retail Prices introduced in June 1947, which was based on the 1937-8 budgets with some adjustment to post-war conditions.[12] A comparison of the weighting given to the main groups of items in 1904, 1937-8, and 1947 reveals the major changes which had taken place in working-class consumption:

ITEMS	1904%	1937-8%	1947%
Food	60	41	34.8
Rent & Rates	16	13	8.8
Clothing	12	9	9.7
Fuel and Light	8	7	6.5
Miscellaneous	4	30	40.2

Before it ceased to be used the 1904/14 index was overweighting food by at least 50 per cent. According to this index food prices had risen between 1914 and 1945 by 69.5 per cent, while the other items had risen by 191 per cent. The index numbers for the two groups were 169.5 and 291. Given the 1904 weighting of food at 60 per cent, the overall rise in cost-of-living index was 118.1 per cent in 1945, an index figure of 218.1.

The sum is: 60 x 169.5 (= 10,170) + 40 x 291 (= 11,640) ÷ 100 = 218.1

The real weighting given to food should have been nearer 40 per cent, which more accurately reflects the true rise in the cost of living at 142.4 per cent, an index figure of 242.4.

The sum is: 40 x 169.5 (= 6,780) + 60 x 291 (= 17,460) ÷ 100 = 242.4

So the outdated cost-of-living index underestimated the rise in the actual cost of living by at least 10 per cent. The 1947 index reveals an even larger shift away from food, rents, and fuel and light towards the 'miscellaneous' group of items. This 40.2 per cent was, incidentally, subdivided into:

Drink and tobacco	21.7%
Services	7.9%
Household durable goods	7.1%
Miscellaneous	3.5%

It has been reliably calculated that, while the 1904/14 cost-of-living index showed a rise between 1938 and 1947 of 29-30 per cent, the rise measured by the two more reliable indexes was between 62 and 73 per cent.

Between 1947 and 1962 four indexes of retail prices were introduced by successive governments, based on estimates of consumption at different dates. From 1962 the weights given to each item were adjusted each year. This means that the current index, in use since 1962, is the first example of a moving target, as it were. No longer does the index measure the current cost of buying a packet of goods which represented an average working-class family's consumption at some earlier date. What is now measured is the cost of buying what the average family in fact buys. From 1975 this is based on expenditure in 'the latest available year'. The other change is that the working-class family's consumption is no longer measured, but that of all families excluding a few very rich households and some of the poorest (*see* p. 55).

WHERE'S THE MYSTERY?

1839.

1879.

FARMERS COULD LIVE THEN.

Value of Produce :—Oats. 17*s.* 6*d.* per qr. ; Barley, 23*s.* 6*d.* per qr. ; Wheat, 13*s.* 6*d.* per bag ; Cheese, 42*s.* 6*d.* per cwt.

FARMERS CAN'T LIVE NOW.

Value of Produce :—Oats, 26*s.* per qr. ; Barley, 45*s.* per qr. ; Wheat, 24*s.* per bag ; Cheese, 80*s.* per cwt.

Conflicting evidence: 1879, an agricultural 'depression', but prices and expectations higher. From *Punch* (early 1880).

This new 'average' family is just as much an illusion as earlier cost-of-living indexes were. The problem is that changes in the cost of living affect different social groups differently. The earlier indexes only covered one social group; the current one amalgamates differing groups. Dudley Seers calculated that between 1938 and 1949 the cost of living for the working-class rose by 82 per cent, while that for the middle-class rose by 102 per cent.[13] To maintain the same relative standards of living, middle-class incomes would need to have risen much more than working-class incomes. The National Consumer Council's Annual Report for 1976-7 revealed the opposite development:

> the buying-power gap between rich and poor had widened because prices of essentials, which take up a bigger proportion of the poor's earnings, have gone up faster than other prices. Whereas in 1968 poorer families could afford £1.41 worth of goods for every £10 worth that richer families could buy, by 1974 that had fallen to £1.31 worth.[14]

The process of change continued:

> 'The earnings gap between the highest and lowest earners has increased over time: for men the gap between those at the bottom and top decile points [point one tenth from the bottom or top of the earnings table] was £203 in 1971, rising to almost £402 in 1994; for women the increase was not as large, £118 in 1971 compared with £279 in 1994'.

This had the consequence that in 1991-2, 'people in the bottom quintile group [bottom fifth] spent a high proportion of their household income on necessities such as food, fuel and housing which accounted for almost half of their spending. In contrast, the top quintile group spent just under a third of their income on these items'.[15]

Indexes measuring wages and standards of living

If we wish to measure how living standards change over time, how far the standard of living rises or falls, then we have to relate changes in the cost of living to changes in income available. An index of what are called 'real wages', that is of how much more or less a money wage will buy in a given year, is produced by a simple mathematical calculation. With a cost-of-living index and a money-wage index having the same base year, the index figure for wages in any other year is divided by the cost-of-living index for the same year. The result, multiplied by 100, is the index number of real wages for that year. Examples taken from an index covering the years 1920-38, with the average of the 12 months of 1924 as 100, will show how the calculation is made.[16] What the following examples reveal is that high money wages do not necessarily mean a higher standard of living.

1920

weekly money wage rate	154.8	
cost of living	151.4	
weekly real wages	102.0	(154.8 ÷ 151.4 = 1.022 x 100=102)

By 1931 the money wage had fallen, but the cost of living (the prices of goods) had fallen more, so real wages (the standard of living) had risen:

1931

weekly money wage rate	95.7	
cost of living	84.0	
weekly real wages	114.0	(95.7 ÷ 84.0 = 1.139 x 100 = 114)

We have much more comprehensive and more reliable information as to money wages

Undoubtedly, and particularly in such heavy work as is found in oil-seed press work and tannery processes, the acquisition of men's rates of pay has had a peculiarly enheartening and stimulating effect. "The difficulty at present," says Miss Vines, " is not so much in direct substitution as in the replacement of women who have left the so-called women's (and lower paid) industries to take a hand in work formerly done by men." Reports from the north-eastern coast towns indicate that introduction there, where no typical women's industry existed before the war, of women as substitutes in shipyards, iron and chemical works, munition factories, has revolutionised the position of women. The average pre-war rate for them was not above 10/- to 12/-, and "it has now risen to a substantially higher level than in the West Riding texile districts—essentially a women's industrial centre." (Miss Lennard.) In a few cases there are complaints of very low wages, and. women replacing men in bottle works were said to be earning only 11/- a week. "Where women are considered unsatisfactory I have generally found that the standard of comfort or of wages has been too low to attract a competent worker. There are still some employers who fail to realise that it is only the rougher kind of women who will go through the streets with the marks of her trade upon her." (Miss Pearson.)

Factory Inspectors' Reports reveal changes in women's wages during the 1914-18 war. From *The Annual Report of the Chief Inspector of Factories and Workshops*, 1916, Cd 8570 (1917), p. 6.

in the 20th century than for earlier periods, so it is possible to calculate the average money wage and to produce indexes which are more reliable than earlier ones. They are, however, only an average of all wages and how unreal this is will appear from an example. In 1931 the weekly wage of an agricultural labourer was 31s. 4d., of a building labourer 51s. 10d., of a shipwright 60s.[17]

In all these calculations we have assumed that there is only one way of measuring money wages, but government statistics differentiate between wage rates and earnings. Wage rates, per hour or week, were in the main those arranged by organisations of employers and workpeople, or by statutory wages councils or boards. They were the agreed payments for an agreed working week. These are reasonably comparable with the figures for wages available for periods before 1914. They do NOT represent what is actually earned in a week. The other set of figures, of earnings, 'represents the average earnings, including bonus, overtime, etc.'. This is clearly a more reliable figure from which to reckon changes in the real standard of living of wage-earners. Unfortunately the official figures are 'before deduction of income tax or insurance contributions'.[18]

Even if we had information as to the net earnings of a sufficient number and variety of people to calculate an average, this would still be an imperfect figure against which to calculate real changes in the standard of living of real people. Most people do not live as individuals but as families, whether joined by legal ties or not. This means that their standard of living is determined by the total family income. Students of poverty in the 20th century have therefore based their investigations and calculations on the family unit. Seebohm Rowntree, in his pioneering *Poverty*, explained that the 'family income' included:

Total wages of father

Total wages of mother

Total wages of any children who are earning not more than 7s. each.

Estimated payment for board and lodging given to their parents by older children.

Payments by lodgers (if any) for board and lodging, the lodgers being counted as members of the family.

Rowntree then ascertained 'the standard of comfort attainable' for the whole family with this total income.[19] In his later study, *Poverty and Progress*, Rowntree used the same classification of family income, though he was more sophisticated in how he applied it to classify levels of poverty.[20] This is not relevant to the purpose of this book. What is relevant is that by studying how Rowntree and other students of poverty made their calculations, we see quite clearly the limitations of measuring change in the living standards of real people by an index based on a wage rate and a cost-of-living index. Since these are the *only* indexes available which cover any long period of time, however, we must make what use we can of them, remembering that they can only indicate trends and do NOT give precise answers to specific cases.

Some examples of actual prices paid for particular items

It has been argued throughout this booklet that indexes have to be used because comparable and exact prices of particular things are unobtainable for long periods of time, or else so limited in scope that they cannot be used generally. A few examples of what this means in practice, from the present writer's experience, may be worth giving before describing the available indexes. A study of the household accounts of two great Hertfordshire families in the 1630s showed that, while the prices of some foodstuffs were quite stable, others changed erratically. Not surprisingly London prices were always more than those at Hertfordshire markets.[21] Ordinary beer cost 6s. a barrel in Hertfordshire and London from 1634 to 1638, but the price of a chicken oscillated between 3½d. and 1s.4d. A stone of beef cost 1s.6d. in the country, but 1s.9d. in London, and a pound of butter 5d. – 6d. in the country and 6d. – 6^1/₂d. in London. Similar sets of accounts have been published in many counties from which local historians may obtain local price levels. More widely available in print are the inventories made in proving wills. The objects listed, furniture and farm goods almost universally, trade goods in many cases, were valued by neighbours at what might be described as local second-hand prices. The valuations, even in one place at a given period, are only too often extremely erratic, though they may give a few clues as to the prices of some possessions in each of the main socio-economic groups.

As for wages, from the late 16th to the early 18th century justices of the peace fixed official wage rates for their counties. You can usually find these tables of wage rates among the quarter sessions records. In Hertfordshire the first surviving table is in the records of the 1589-90 session; the last one available was in 1708. These tables go into a great deal of detail, distinguishing payments 'with meat and drink' provided by the employer from payments 'without meat and drink', for each of many categories of agricultural workers and 'artificers': 'the best sort', 'the second sort' and 'the worst sort' in each category were to be paid differently, and women's wages were given for some occupations. The rates were raised from time to time. A considerable advance in 1687 led to the complaint that 'the licentious humours of some servants ... have advanced ... their wages and the expense of their diet above the rents of their masters' farms', which has quite a modern ring.[22] The common labourer's daily wage rose from 8d. in summer and 7d. in winter to 10d. in 1687.

These were intended to be maximum rates, but were they the actual wages paid?

" SERVANTS WAGES."
" Servants of Husbandry by the year."

	£	s.	d.
" A Bailif having meat and drink ...	6	0	0
The Chiefe Ploughman having meat and drink	6	0	0
The second Ploughman or Carter having meat and drink	5	0	0
The Horse-Keeper having meat and drink	3	10	0
The Shepherd or Neatherd having meat and drink	4	0	0
The Tasker having meat and drink ...	6	0	0
The Under Tasker or Odd Man	5	0	0
The Gardener having meat and drink ...	6	0	0
But if any of theis servants have no meat and drink, then they may have in lieu thereof, over and above the said wages, per year	8	0	0
The Chamber Maid by the year	3	0	0
The Wash Maid by the year	2	10	0
The Dairy Maid by the year	2	10	0
The Cooke Maid by the year	2	10	0

Labourers in Hay.

	£	s.	d.
For Mowing of Grass by the day... ...	0	1	2
For Mowing of Grass by the acre ...	0	1	6
For a Man that shall make Hay by the day	0	0	10
For a Woman that shall make Hay by the day	0	0	4
For makeing Hay by the acre	0	1	6

Labourers in Harvest.

	£	s.	d.
The Man Reaper by the day haveing meat and drink	0	1	0
Haveing no meat and drink	0	1	6
The Woman Reaper by the day haveing meat and drink	0	0	8
Haveing no meat and drink	0	1	2
For Reaping, Binding and Shocking Wheat, Rye or Misline by the acre ...	0	4	0
For Mowing of Barly, Oates or Bully-mong and Cocking the same by the acre	0	1	6
For Reaping and Binding of Beanes by the acre	0	3	0
For Hooking of Pease, Fitches or Tares by the acre	0	1	6
For working the whole Harvest, with meat and drink	1	10	0

Legally-binding wages fixed by Hertfordshire Quarter Sessions in the late 17th century. From *Hertfordshire County Records. Calendar to the Sessions Books 1658-1700*, Vol. VI (1930), p.400. Reproduced by permission of the former County Archivist, Peter Walne.

Wages paid may be found in various contemporary records: churchwardens' accounts, estate records and the accounts of large households are most likely to produce evidence. In 1605 Knebworth's churchwardens paid two labourers 1s. 4d. 'for one day's work'.[23] This was the maximum payment fixed by Quarter Sessions. Casual male workers at Gorhambury, employed inside and outside the house in 1637-9, were paid 10d. a day, women workers 6d.[24] The rate of wages fixed by St. Albans magistrates in 1632 was 10d. a day in the summer and 8d. in the winter for men; no rates were fixed for women's casual work. Higher rates were paid to 'artificers', that is craftsmen. The rate current in the 1590s was: 'freemasons, carpenters, joiners, wheelwrights, plowrights, bricklayers, tilers and plasterers, being masters of the said occupations or of the best sort shall not have more by the day' than 11d. in the winter, 1s. in the summer, without meat and drink. The 'second sort' were to be paid not more than 8d. or 10d. Between 1591 and 1593 the churchwardens of St Peter's, St Albans, paid 1s. a day to a carpenter, a tiler and 'Fuller the workman', but only 8d to their and other artificers' men.[25] This was the summer rate for 'the worst sort'.

The first example of payments substantially over the legal maximum is for artificers employed at Gorhambury in 1637-8. The 1632 St. Albans magistrates' rate for artificers in the same categories as listed in the 1590s was 1s.4d. a day, 1s. 2d. for the second sort, and 10d. for the worst sort. At Gorhambury masons, glaziers and carpenters were paid between 1s. 4d. and 1s. 6d., bricklayers and joiners 1s. 6d. to 1s.8d. Their 'servers' or 'men' were paid 1s.[26]

Since the tables of wages fixed by magistrates list the wage 'with meat and drink' and 'without', we have a figure for the assumed cost of feeding a man for a day. This was 4d. in most cases for men, but 3d. or even 2d. for women. Exceptionally, before 1632, thatchers' servants in the summer were paid only 3d. In the 1632 list labourers in the summer and artificers of the worst sort were to be paid 5d., and those of the second sort 6d. When the Cecils moved house in the 1630s they paid some servants for their board: these superior servants were paid 5s. a week, which is about 8½d. a day. A few people were paid more. Three of the lower staff were each paid 6d. a day, 'having diet' when on the move. Two more, without diet or lodging, were paid 9d. each.[27] The 1687 table raised the cost of a day's feeding to 6d. for labourers, whether men or women, but left the gardener's rate at 4d! For most occupations only a rate 'having meat and drink' was given.

It needs to be remembered that for much of the time, in the Middle Ages and until the early modern period, a large number of people employed as 'servants of husbandry' were 'living in' and being maintained in the farmer's household, as well as receiving wages. In some cases they also received a 'livery', defined in 1632 as a coat and a yard and a half of broadcloth for a manservant; this was valued at 10s. though the broadcloth to be provided, it was specified, should cost 8s. or 9s. a yard![28] In the case of board and lodging we are, unusually, able to give a reasonably equivalent modern parallel. The Agricultural Wages Order of 1995 (AWB No 3, p 15) prints 'the values at which benefits were reckonable in part payment of [agricultural labourers'] wages at the minimum rates'. These were, for a seven days' week: £56.04 for board and lodging, £46.70 for board only. The £46.70 of 1995 is a 400 times increase on the 4d. a day, which becomes 2s. 4d. for 7 days, paid for 'meat and drink' in Hertfordshire in the 1590s. £56.04 is 213.5 times the 9d. (5s. 3d. for 7 days) which Cecil paid in the 1630s for 'diet and lodging'.

An entirely different comparison, which shows much less change over time, is of the

An extract from the probate inventory of a Carlisle shopkeeper, Robert Patinson, appraised in 1571, showing some of the variety of goods he sold. Cloth constituted the bulk of his stock. Reproduced by permission of Cumbria County Record Office, Carlisle (P1571).

relationship between the purchase price of land and rents in seventeenth and late twentieth century Hertfordshire. This comparison is based on an extremely limited number of examples, but it is suggestive. Seventeenth century rents of arable land were c.5% of purchase price, twentieth century ones 3%-3.7%.

Information like this can be collected from similar sources, and many others, in most English counties. It can give us precise evidence for changes in prices and wages over short periods of time, in particular areas, and for a limited range of goods and people. Occasional comparisons between then and now may be possible, but to calculate the changes in intervening years we would need to accumulate an enormous mass of disparate detail and employ a computer and programmers for years. This is where our indexes come in, but particular local prices should be used, where available, as a check on calculations based on indexes.

For the late 18th century we have specific examples of family budgeting from many English counties. Sir Frederick Eden described the actual expenditure and total earnings of particular families in various parts of the country in about 1795. The yearly expenses of a Berkshire labourer's family of six (man, wife, and four children of ages of five, seven, 12 and 14) were:

	£	s.	d.
8 half-peck loaves a week, or 410 in the year, at 1s. 9d.	36	8	0
2lb of cheese a week, at 7d. per lb	3	0	8
2lb of butter a week, at 9d. per lb	3	18	0
2lb of sugar a week, at 9d. per lb	3	18	0

		£	s.	d.
2oz of tea a week, at 3s. per lb			19	6
¹/₂lb of oatmeal a week, at 3d. per lb			6	6
¹/₂lb of bacon a week, at 3d. per lb		3	5	0
2d. in milk every week			8	8
		52	4	4

In Westmorland a labourer's family of five (man, wife, and three children of ages one, two and four) bought in a year:

	£	s.	d.
75 stone of oatmeal	8	15	0
Butcher's meat and flour		5	0
Milk	5	0	0
Tea and sugar	1	12	0
Potatoes	2	12	0
Butter, 40lbs at 9d. per lb	1	10	0
Treacle		8	0
	20	2	0

The differences in diet are significant, but so is something else. The Berkshire family spent more than twice as much as the Westmorland family, on what may have been a less healthy diet. Though better paid they were £17 18s. 8d. short of what they needed to pay their living expenses in the year.[29] For the same areas it should not be impossible to get comparable food prices and labourers' family earnings for an earlier date in the 18th century. Similar exercises may be possible in other places, *but* for most of the country, for most periods, and for any substantial range of occupations, such information is not available. The indexes are our only guide.

In the second part of this book, which follows, we publish a selection of indexes, covering the period from the 1200s until today, with descriptions of how each one was compiled and some suggestions as to its consequent limitations.

Above: A shop in the Market Place, St Albans about 1930.

Left: Symington & Son of Market Place, St Albans in 1897. Described as 'clothiers, tailors and juvenile outfitters; sole agents for Vine & Co's Butchers clothings.'

Reproduced by permission of St Albans Museums.

STATISTICAL APPENDIX

PRE–20TH CENTURY INDEXES

MEDIEVAL TO MODERN.

Phelps Brown and Hopkins

This covers the longest period of time (1264-1954) of any of the indexes and begins at the earliest date. It is based on a 'composite unit of consumables'. The compilers, E. H. Phelps Brown and Sheila V. Hopkins, have explained that this is *not* a real cost-of-living index because little is known about important costs, such as rent, and the prices available are wholesale rather than retail. They are, in the main, compiled from contract prices paid by institutions. They are *not*, so to say, prices paid over the counter. The compilers in any case make it clear they 'could not attach much meaning to "the cost of maintaining a constant standard of living" through seven centuries of social change'. So their index is of the 'aggregate price year by year for a composite commodity, made up always of the same amounts of some of the main heads of consumption'. The composite unit has six 'bags' or groups of consumables: farinaceous, meat and fish, butter and cheese, drink, fuel and light, textiles. 'The contents of each bag have been made up variously from time to time: in our breadstuffs, for instance, we give a greater place to wheat, and correspondingly less to rye and barley, as the eighteenth century wears on'. The base period chosen

> is 1451-75, because it lies within a long period of stability in the trend of prices ..... The index of prices has two periods, each of about 130 years, 1380-1510, and 1630-1760, throughout which there is constancy in the general level .... The most marked feature .... is the extent, and persistence, of the Tudor inflation.[30]

What this index does provide, over a very long period of time, is a rough measure of change against which particular local changes in the price of individual objects can be considered.

The index of the wage-rate of building craftsmen which parallels the index of consumables was compiled from several sources, which are explained by the authors. Basically the wages are drawn from southern England, and particularly from the area around Oxford, while the prices of consumables apply to southern England generally. Until the early 19th century prices are those paid by institutions buying in bulk; thereafter wholesale, not retail, prices have been used.

Column (1) *Composite unit of consumables 1264-1954*
Column (2) *Wage-rate of building craftsmen, expressed in the composite unit 1264-1954*
1451-75 = 100

	1	2		1	2		1	2		1	2		1	2
1260	-	-	1310	135	-	1360	135	61	1410	130	-	1460	97	103
1261	-	-	1311	123	54	1361	131	63	1411	106	-	1461	117	85
1262	-	-	1312	108	62	1362	153	54	1412	103	97	1462	115	87
1263	-	-	1313	101	66	1363	155	54	1413	108	93	1463	88	114
1264	83	60	1314	112	60	1364	151	55	1414	108	93	1464	86	116
1265	80	63	1315	132	51	1365	143	58	1415	115	87	1465	108	93
1266	83	60	1316	216	31	1366	121	69	1416	124	81	1466	109	92
1267	-	-	1317	215	31	1367	137	61	1417	129	78	1467	108	93
1268	70	71	1318	154	44	1368	139	60	1418	114	88	1468	106	94
1269	83	60	1319	119	56	1369	150	55	1419	95	105	1469	107	93
1270	-	-	1320	106	63	1370	184	45	1420	102	98	1470	102	98
1271	98	51	1321	121	55	1371	164	51	1421	93	108	1471	103	97
1272	130	38	1322	141	48	1372	132	63	1422	97	103	1472	104	96
1273	98	51	1323	165	41	1373	131	63	1423	108	93	1473	97	103
1274	95	53	1324	137	49	1374	125	66	1424	103	97	1474	95	105
1275	100	50	1325	127	53	1375	125	66	1425	109	92	1475	90	111
1276	96	52	1326	124	54	1376	146	57	1426	103	97	1476	85	118
1277	97	52	1327	96	70	1377	112	74	1427	96	104	1477	81	123
1278	103	49	1328	96	70	1378	95	87	1428	99	101	1478	89	112
1279	94	53	1329	119	56	1379	94	88	1429	127	79	1479	97	103
1280	94	53	1330	120	56	1380	106	78	1430	138	72	1480	103	97
1281	93	54	1331	134	50	1381	119	70	1431	115	87	1481	115	87
1282	104	48	1332	131	51	1382	111	75	1432	102	98	1482	145	69
1283	111	45	1333	111	60	1383	108	77	1433	112	89	1483	162	62
1284	120	42	1334	99	68	1384	116	72	1434	109	98	1484	128	78
1285	83	60	1335	96	70	1385	112	74	1435	105	95	1485	99	101
1286	91	55	1336	101	66	1386	104	80	1436	95	105	1486	86	116
1287	91	55	1337	111	60	1387	100	83	1437	93	108	1487	103	97
1288	72	69	1338	85	-	1388	102	81	1438	128	78	1488	110	90
1289	69	72	1339	79	-	1389	100	83	1439	154	65	1489	109	92
1290	80	63	1340	96	52	1390	106	78	1440	140	71	1490	106	94
1291	106	47	1341	86	58	1391	133	62	1441	93	108	1491	112	89
1292	96	52	1342	85	59	1392	104	80	1442	85	118	1492	103	97
1293	93	54	1343	84	60	1393	100	83	1443	97	103	1493	117	85
1294	110	45	1344	97	52	1394	101	82	1444	102	98	1494	96	104
1295	131	38	1345	98	51	1395	93	89	1445	87	115	1495	89	112
1296	104	48	1346	88	57	1396	99	84	1446	95	105	1496	94	106
1297	93	54	1347	109	46	1397	116	72	1447	100	100	1497	101	99
1298	106	47	1348	116	43	1398	121	69	1448	102	98	1498	96	104
1299	96	52	1349	97	52	1399	113	73	1449	106	94	1499	99	101
1300	113	44	1350	102	49	1400	104	80	1450	102	98	1500	94	106
1301	89	-	1351	134	-	1401	130	64	1451	109	92	1501	107	93
1302	93	-	1352	160	-	1402	127	65	1452	97	103	1502	122	82
1303	89	-	1353	138	-	1403	119	-	1453	97	103	1503	114	88
1304	94	62	1354	117	-	1404	99	-	1454	105	95	1504	107	93
1305	97	60	1355	115	-	1405	99	-	1455	94	106	1505	103	97
1306	100	58	1356	121	-	1406	100	-	1456	102	99	1506	106	94
1307	94	62	1357	133	-	1407	99	-	1447	93	108	1507	98	102
1308	105	55	1358	139	-	1408	107	-	1458	99	101	1508	100	100
1309	119	-	1359	126	-	1409	120	-	1459	95	105	1509	92	109

	1	2		1	2		1	2		1	2		1	2
1510	103	97	1560	265	-	1610	503	40	1660	684	44	1710	798	46
1511	97	103	1561	283	59	1611	463	43	1661	648	46	1711	889	41
1512	101	99	1562	266	63	1612	524	38	1662	769	46	1712	638	58
1513	120	83	1563	-	-	1613	549	36	1663	675	44	1713	594	62
1514	118	85	1564	-	-	1614	567	35	1664	657	46	1714	635	58
1515	107	93	1565	290	58	1615	561	36	1665	616	49	1715	646	57
1516	110	90	1566	287	58	1616	562	36	1666	664	45	1716	645	57
1517	111	90	1567	282	59	1617	537	37	1667	577	52	1717	602	61
1518	116	86	1568	281	59	1618	524	38	1668	602	50	1718	575	64
1519	120	78	1569	276	61	1619	494	40	1669	572	52	1719	609	60
1520	137	73	1570	300	56	1620	485	41	1670	577	52	1720	635	58
1521	167	60	1571	265	63	1621	461	43	1671	595	50	1721	604	61
1522	160	63	1572	270	62	1622	523	38	1672	557	54	1722	554	66
1523	136	74	1573	274	61	1623	588	34	1673	585	51	1723	525	70
1524	133	75	1574	374	-	1624	543	37	1674	650	46	1724	589	62
1525	129	78	1575	-	-	1625	534	37	1675	691	43	1725	610	60
1526	133	75	1576	309	-	1626	552	36	1676	652	46	1726	637	58
1527	147	68	1577	363	-	1627	496	40	1677	592	51	1727	596	62
1528	179	56	1578	351	-	1628	466	43	1678	633	47	1728	649	57
1529	159	63	1579	326	-	1629	510	39	1679	614	49	1729	681	54
1530	169	59	1580	342	58	1630	595	-	1680	568	53	1730	599	61
1531	154	65	1581	347	58	1631	682	-	1681	567	53	1731	553	-
1532	179	56	1582	343	58	1632	580	-	1682	600	50	1732	557	-
1533	169	-	1583	324	62	1633	565	-	1683	587	51	1733	544	-
1534	145	-	1584	333	60	1634	611	-	1684	570	53	1734	518	-
1535	131	-	1585	338	59	1635	597	-	1685	651	46	1735	529	-
1536	164	-	1586	352	57	1636	593	-	1686	559	54	1736	539	74
1537	155	-	1587	491	41	1637	621	-	1687	580	52	1737	581	69
1538	138	-	1588	346	58	1638	707	-	1688	551	-	1738	563	71
1539	147	-	1589	354	56	1639	607	-	1689	535	-	1739	547	73
1540	158	-	1590	396	51	1640	546	-	1690	513	-	1740	644	62
1541	165	-	1591	459	44	1641	586	-	1691	493	-	1741	712	56
1542	172	-	1592	370	54	1642	557	48	1692	542	-	1742	631	63
1543	171	-	1593	356	56	1643	553	-	1693	652	-	1743	579	69
1544	178	-	1594	381	52	1644	531	-	1694	693	-	1744	518	77
1545	191	-	1595	515	39	1645	574	-	1695	645	-	1745	528	76
1546	248	-	1596	505	40	1646	569	-	1696	697	-	1746	594	67
1547	231	-	1597	685	29	1647	667	-	1697	693	-	1747	574	70
1548	193	61	1598	579	35	1648	770	-	1698	767	-	1748	599	67
1549	214	-	1599	474	42	1649	821	-	1699	773	-	1749	609	66
1550	262	-	1600	459	44	1650	839	-	1700	671	-	1750	590	68
1551	285	-	1601	536	37	1651	704	-	1701	586	57	1751	574	70
1552	276	48	1602	471	42	1652	648	-	1702	582	-	1752	601	67
1553	259	-	1603	448	45	1653	579	-	1703	551	-	1753	585	68
1554	276	-	1604	404	50	1654	543	-	1704	587	-	1754	615	65
1555	270	-	1605	448	45	1655	531	56	1705	548	-	1755	578	69
1556	370	-	1606	468	43	1656	559	54	1706	583	-	1756	602	66
1557	409	-	1607	449	45	1657	612	49	1707	531	-	1757	733	55
1558	230	-	1608	507	39	1658	646	46	1708	571	-	1758	731	55
1559	255	-	1609	559	36	1659	700	43	1709	697	-	1759	673	59

	1	2		1	2		1	2		1	2		1	2
1760	643	62	1800	1567	38	1840	1286	62	1880	1174	102	1920	2591	154
1761	614	65	1801	1751	34	1841	1256	64	1881	1213	99	1921	2048	167
1762	638	63	1802	1348	45	1842	1161	69	1882	1140	105	1922	1672	164
1763	655	61	1803	1268	-	1843	1030	78	1883	1182	102	1923	1726	159
1764	713	56	1804	1309	-	1844	1029	78	1884	1071	112	1924	1740	172
1765	738	54	1805	1521	-	1845	1079	74	1885	1026	117	1925	1708	176
1766	747	54	1806	1454	49	1846	1122	71	1886	931	129	1926	1577	190
1767	790	51	1807	1427	50	1847	1257	65	1887	955	126	1927	1496	201
1768	781	51	1808	1476	49	1848	1105	74	1888	950	126	1928	1485	202
1769	717	56	1809	1619	44	1849	1035	79	1889	948	127	1929	1511	199
1770	714	56	1810	1670	48	1850	969	84	1890	947	127	1930	1275	229
1771	775	52	1811	1622	49	1851	961	85	1891	998	120	1931	1146	247
1772	858	47	1812	1836	44	1852	978	84	1892	996	120	1932	1065	266
1773	855	47	1813	1881	43	1853	1135	79	1893	914	137	1933	1107	248
1774	863	-	1814	1642	49	1854	1265	71	1894	982	127	1934	1097	251
1775	815	-	1815	1467	55	1855	1274	71	1895	968	129	1935	1149	254
1776	797	61	1816	1344	60	1856	1264	71	1896	947	132	1936	1211	248
1777	794	61	1817	1526	52	1857	1287	70	1897	963	130	1937	1275	242
1778	826	58	1818	1530	52	1858	1190	76	1898	982	127	1938	1274	249
1779	756	64	1819	1492	54	1859	1214	74	1899	950	140	1939	1209	269
1780	730	66	1820	1353	59	1860	1314	68	1900	994	134	1940	1574	222
1781	760	64	1821	1190	67	1861	1302	72	1901	986	135	1911	1784	206
1782	776	62	1822	1029	78	1862	1290	72	1902	963	138	1942	2130	176
1783	869	56	1823	1099	73	1863	1144	82	1903	1004	133	1943	2145	183
1784	874	55	1824	1193	67	1864	1200	78	1904	985	135	1944	2216	184
1785	839	58	1825	1400	57	1865	1238	-	1905	989	135	1945	2282	186
1786	889	58	1826	1323	60	1866	1296	82	1906	1016	131	1946	2364	208
1787	834	58	1827	1237	65	1867	1346	79	1907	1031	129	1947	2580	210
1788	867	56	1828	1201	67	1868	1291	82	1908	1043	128	1948	2781	198
1789	856	56	1829	1189	67	1869	1244	86	1909	1058	126	1949	3145	178
1790	871	55	1830	1146	70	1870	1241	86	1910	994	134	1950	3155	180
1791	870	55	1831	1260	63	1871	1320	81	1911	984	135	1951	3656	170
1792	883	-	1832	1167	69	1872	1378	-	1912	999	133	1952	3987	167
1793	908	-	1833	1096	73	1873	1437	84	1913	1021	131	1953	3735	187
1794	978	-	1834	1011	79	1874	1423	84	1914	1147	124	1954	3825	194
1795	1091	-	1835	1028	78	1875	1310	92	1915	1317	114	-	-	-
1796	1161	52	1836	1141	70	1876	1370	88	1916	1652	94	-	-	-
1797	1045	57	1837	1169	68	1877	1330	90	1917	1965	87	-	-	-
1798	1022	59	1838	1177	68	1878	1281	94	1918	2497	80	-	-	-
1799	1148	52	1839	1263	63	1879	1210	99	1919	2254	126	-	-	-

('Seven Centuries of the Prices of Consumables...' in *Economica* (1956), reprinted in *Essays in Economic History*, vol. 2, edited by E. M. Carus Wilson (1962), pp. 193-6)

Bank of England: Equivalent contemporary values of the pound: historical series 1270 to 1992.

This statistical series shows changes in the value of money over the past seven centuries and gives the amount of money required at October 1992 to purchase the goods bought by £1 at the dates shown on the table. Thus, £66.62 would have been required in October 1992 in order to have the same purchasing power as £1 in 1690.

The figures are derived from the Retail Price Index, based at January 1987 =100. There are no figures for individual years before 1800. This Bank of England series is statistically accurate but, as has been explained earlier especially on pp 17-20, cannot be used as a simple multiplier applied to any particular money sum in the past. The money equivalents are, in effect, abstractions.

Year	Value	Year	Value	Year	Value	Year	Value
1270	£349.75	1570	£127.18	1807	£27.43	1837	£33.31
1280	£349.75	1580	£139.90	1808	£26.40	1838	£32.53
1290	£466.33	1590	£116.58	1809	£23.71	1839	£30.41
1300	£349.75	1600	£99.93	1810	£23.32	1840	£30.41
1310	£349.75	1610	£73.63	1811	£23.71	1841	£31.09
1320	£279.80	1620	£73.63	1812	£21.20	1842	£33.31
1330	£349.75	1630	£69.95	1813	£20.57	1843	£37.81
1340	£466.33	1640	£66.62	1814	£23.71	1844	£37.81
1350	£349.75	1650	£58.29	1815	£26.40	1845	£35.87
1360	£279.80	1660	£58.29	1816	£29.15	1846	£34.12
1370	£279.80	1670	£63.59	1817	£25.44	1847	£31.09
1380	£349.75	1680	£63.59	1818	£25.44	1848	£34.97
1390	£349.75	1690	£66.62	1819	£25.91	1849	£37.81
1400	£349.75	1700	£60.83	1820	£28.55	1850	£39.97
1410	£349.75	1710	£58.29	1821	£32.53	1851	£41.15
1420	£349.75	1720	£63.59	1822	£37.81	1852	£41.15
1430	£349.75	1730	£66.62	1823	£34.97	1853	£37.81
1440	£349.75	1740	£66.62	1824	£32.53	1854	£32.53
1450	£349.75	1750	£66.62	1825	£27.98	1855	£31.80
1460	£349.75	1760	£58.29	1826	£29.15	1856	£31.80
1470	£349.75	1770	£48.24	1827	£31.09	1857	£33.31
1480	£349.75	1780	£48.24	1828	£32.53	1858	£36.82
1490	£349.75	1790	£43.72	1829	£32.53	1859	£36.82
1500	£349.75	1800	£24.54	1830	£34.12	1860	£35.87
1510	£349.75	1801	£22.21	1831	£31.09	1861	£34.97
1520	£349.75	1802	£28.55	1832	£33.31	1862	£35.87
1530	£279.80	1803	£30.41	1833	£34.97	1863	£36.82
1540	£233.17	1804	£29.77	1834	£37.81	1864	£37.81
1550	£233.17	1805	£25.44	1835	£37.81	1865	£36.82
1560	£155.44	1806	£26.90	1836	£34.12	1866	£34.97

Year		Value	Year		Value	Year		Value	Year		Value
1867	-	£33.31	1902	-	£43.72	1937	-	£24.98	1972	-	£6.45
1868	-	£33.31	1903	-	£43.72	1938	-	£24.98	1973	-	£5.90
1869	-	£34.97	1904	-	£43.72	1939	-	£24.54	1974	-	£5.09
1870	-	£34.97	1905	-	£43.72	1940	-	£21.20	1975	-	£4.10
1871	-	£34.97	1906	-	£46.63	1941	-	£19.43	1976	-	£3.52
1872	-	£33.31	1907	-	£42.39	1942	-	£19.43	1977	-	£3.03
1873	-	£32.53	1908	-	£41.15	1943	-	£19.43	1978	-	£2.80
1874	-	£34.12	1909	-	£41.15	1944	-	£19.43	1979	-	£2.47
1875	-	£34.97	1910	-	£41.15	1945	-	£19.16	1980	-	£2.09
1876	-	£35.87	1911	-	£39.97	1946	-	£18.91	1981	-	£1.87
1877	-	£34.97	1912	-	£38.86	1947	-	£18.91	1982	-	£1.72
1878	-	£35.87	1913	-	£38.86	1948	-	£17.71	1983	-	£1.65
1879	-	£38.86	1914	-	£38.86	1949	-	£17.27	1984	-	£1.57
1880	-	£36.82	1915	-	£31.09	1950	-	£16.65	1985	-	£1.48
1881	-	£37.81	1916	-	£26.40	1951	-	£15.37	1986	-	£1.43
1882	-	£37.81	1917	-	£21.86	1952	-	£13.99	1987	-	£1.37
1883	-	£38.86	1918	-	£17.94	1953	-	£13.58	1988	-	£1.31
1884	-	£39.97	1919	-	£17.94	1954	-	£13.32	1989	-	£1.21
1885	-	£42.39	1920	-	£15.54	1955	-	£12.83	1990	-	£1.11
1886	-	£43.72	1921	-	£17.06	1956	-	£12.17	1991	-	£1.05
1887	-	£45.13	1922	-	£21.20	1957	-	£11.76			
1888	-	£45.13	1923	-	£22.21	1958	-	£11.47			
1889	-	£43.72	1924	-	£22.21	1959	-	£11.37			
1890	-	£43.72	1925	-	£21.86	1960	-	£11.28			
1891	-	£43.72	1926	-	£22.56	1961	-	£10.84			
1892	-	£43.72	1927	-	£22.93	1962	-	£10.44			
1893	-	£45.13	1928	-	£23.32	1963	-	£10.21			
1894	-	£46.63	1929	-	£23.71	1964	-	£9.92			
1895	-	£48.24	1930	-	£24.54	1965	-	£9.45			
1896	-	£48.24	1931	-	£26.40	1966	-	£9.08			
1897	-	£46.63	1932	-	£26.90	1967	-	£8.85			
1898	-	£46.63	1933	-	£27.98	1968	-	£8.48			
1899	-	£46.63	1934	-	£27.43	1969	-	£8.04			
1900	-	£45.13	1935	-	£26.90	1970	-	£7.56			
1901	-	£45.13	1936	-	£26.40	1971	-	£6.89			

SIXTEENTH TO SEVENTEENTH CENTURIES

Phelps Brown and Hopkins

Two overlapping indexes cover this period. Phelps Brown and Hopkins have published a more sophisticated measure of change than that revealed by their longer index. It covers the period 1401-1700; we reproduce the table from 1451. The authors were concerned to explain the fall in the purchasing power of builders' wages in the sixteenth century. They explained this by arguing that the population growth affected agricultural and industrial production differently: 'we should not expect agriculture to have the capacity for expansion.. that could raise its labour force or its product proportionately to the rise in population. The overspill of labour would have had to go into. industrial employments. [This led to] changes in the terms of trade between agriculture and industry'.[31] The result is shown in the table which distinguishes between the 'price of a composite unit of foodstuffs' and the 'price of a sample of industrial products'. By 1691-1700 the price of foodstuffs had risen much more than twice that of industrial products.

1451-75 = 100

Dates	Foodstuffs	Industrial products
1451-75	100	100
1491-1500	100	97
1501-10	106	98
1511-20	116	102
1521-30	159	110
1531-40	161	110
1541-50	217	127
1551-60	315	186
1561-70	298	218
1571-80	341	230
1581-90	389	230
1591-1600	530	238
1601-10	527	256
1611-20	583	274
1621-30	585	264
1631-40	687	281
1641-50	723	306
1651-60	687	327
1661-70	702	343
1671-80	675	351
1681-90	631	310
1691-1700	737	331

(E. H. Phelps Brown and S.V. Hopkins, 'Wage-rates and prices',
Economica, vol. 24 (1957), p.306)

Peter Bowden.

Bowden, by combining Thorold Rogers' and Beveridge's figures with those from many other more limited sources, which he lists, has compiled indexes for many different products and for agricultural day wage-rates in southern England. There are index figures for every year, as well as the decennial averages which are printed below. There are separate indexes for the separate products combined in the groups listed below. 'All grains', for example, is the average of separate indexes for wheat, barley, oats and rye. Peter Bowden's comments on the difficulty produced by the lack of 'long series of observations from the same source' are a warning as to the limitations of indexes for this period. For the local historian he has a special warning: 'the concept of an average price level is an abstraction [and] in the conditions of Tudor and early Stuart times prices might vary widely from one local market to another'.[32]

Agricultural commodities: decennial averages 1450-1649
1450-99 = 100

Decade	A	B	C	D	E	F	G	H	I
1450-9	98	96	98	84	97	91	86	96	99
1460-9	99	101	102	103	102	91	110	102	103
1470-9	93	101	108	94	98	105	101	98	100
1480-9	114	99	105	111	105	105	110	106	103
1490-9	97	98	90	103	99	102	101	99	97
1500-9	112	98	103	95	111	93	108	106	98
1510-9	115	120	119	128	117	93	131	118	102
1520-9	154	132	143	138	138	94	115	132	110
1530-9	161	128	147	158	143	109	136	139	110
1540-9	187	145	174	210	185	139	161	169	127
1550-9	348	261	266	263	259	216	210	270	186
1560-9	316	294	290	312	281	225	220	282	218
1570-9	370	288	358	380	336	223	279	313	223
1580-9	454	328	389	392	352	261	305	357	230
1590-9	590	428	465	471	414	313	375	451	238
1600-9	560	454	489	495	451	323	414	463	256
1610-9	655	551	553	525	507	369	472	540	274
1620-9	642	546	545	557	524	354	462	535	264
1630-9	790	660	646	587	630	389	486	634	281
1640-9	786	664	713	681	667	439	460	644	306

A = all grains; B = all other arable crops; C = all cattle; D = all sheep; E = all livestock; F = all dairy products; G = wool, fells & hides; H = all agricultural products; I = all industrial products.

Silver pennies of Edward the Confessor, 1056-66, (*top*) Dover mint, (*bottom*) Chichester mint.

Penny of William I or William II of the so-called PAXS type, struck at Cricklade by the moneyer Aelfwine; photographed (left) and drawn (right).

Date	Agricultural day wage-rates in Southern England Average money wage in pence [d.]	Index Number
1450-9	4.00	101
1460-9	4.00	101
1470-9	4.00	101
1480-9	3.75	95
1490-9	4.00	101
1500-9	4.00	101
1510-9	4.00	101
1520-9	4.17	106
1530-9	4.33	110
1540-9	4.66	118
1550-9	6.33	160
1560-9	7.00	177
1570-9	8.17	207
1580.9	8.00	203
1590-9	8.66	219
1600-9	8.66	219
1610-9	9.00	228
1620-9	10.00	253
1630-0	11.33	287
1640-9	12.00	304

(P. Bowden, 'Note on statistical sources and methods', in Statistical Appendix to *The Agrarian History of England and Wales*, IV, 1500-1640, edited by J. Thirsk (1967), pp. 857-8, 860-2 and 864)

Silver penny of Henry I, 1100-01.

Silver farthing of Edward III, 1335-43.

SEVENTEENTH TO EIGHTEENTH CENTURIES.

Peter Bowden

Peter Bowden has continued his work in a second series of indexes covering the years 1640 to 1749. This can be compared with earlier, overlapping indexes prepared by Elizabeth Gilboy which extend from 1700 to 1796. Bowden found that 'although seventeenth and eighteenth-century agricultural price data are somewhat more plentiful than for earlier periods, there are comparatively few farm products for which we possess continuous time series extending over all, or the larger part, of the period covered'. He discusses other difficulties: 'differences with respect to ... quality, type, condition, age, or weight' of the product; and a 'lack of standardization in the use of weights and measures'. However he developed sophisticated statistical techniques, which he explained, to overcome these difficulties as far as was possible. These are the earliest indexes to be based on 'regional price averages'. The country was divided into nine regions 'to provide geographical balance to our country-wide price indices'. As for wages, 'because of their piecemeal nature, seventeenth- and eighteenth-century wage data are, if anything, more difficult than price data to assemble and integrate into an analytically useful form'.[33] Bowden explains how he dealt with the problems which he met, and lists an impressive range of publications and local records used in compiling his indexes.

Agricultural commodities: decennial averages 1640-1749
1640-1749 =100

Decade	A	B	C	D	E	F	G	H
1640-9	122	101	107	98	85	131	104	97
1650-9	106	104	94	105	93	113	101	103
1660-9	101	88	95	101	93	100	97	109
1670-9	99	91	100	92	94	97	95	111
1680-9	92	103	89	100	98	95	97	98
1690-9	110	105	107	102	109	107	108	105
1700-9	91	96	107	99	108	92	99	103
1710-9	99	108	102	101	107	90	104	97
1720-9	101	100	104	100	105	94	101	93
1730-9	89	102	96	104	107	91	98	89
1740-9	88	104	103	108	108	97	100	93

A = all grains; B = all other field crops; C = all cattle; D = all sheep; E = all livestock; F = all dairy products; G = all agricultural products; H = all industrial products.

Silver groat of Edward III, 1351-61

Silver groat of Edward IV, 1464/5-70.

Agricultural day wage-rates in certain areas of England

Date	Average money wage in pence (d.)	Index number
1640-9	11.00	98
1650-9	11.00	98
1660-9	11.00	98
1670-9	11.00	98
1680-9	11.14	99
1690-9	11.28	100
1700-9	11.12	99
1710-9	11.29	100
1720-9	11.13	99
1730-9	11.64	104
1740-9	12.07	107

(P. Bowden, 'Statistics', in Appendix III of *The Agrarian History of England and Wales, V, 1640-1750, II Agrarian Change*, edited by J. Thirsk (1985), pp. 851-6 and 877 and 879).

Elizabeth Gilboy

Gilboy's cost-of-living index is derived mainly from contract prices and must be regarded as very rough. It relates principally to London and southern England. The years referred to are those beginning at Michaelmas. It is 'a weighted average of price relatives, with 1700 as a base...relating, as far as data permits, to goods which were consumed by the English laborer...The commodities were divided into five groups...with the following weights: cereals, 5; animal products, 2; candles and coal, 1; beverages and condiments, 1; clothing, 1. The weights were determined after a careful study of sample budgets published by Eden and Davies'.* This index was used to estimate the real wages of Lancashire as well as of London. The 'wage indices relate to the weekly wages of men in full employment'. 'The London index is an average of price relatives of the daily wage rates of bricklayers', masons', paviours', and plasterers' labor at Westminster Abbey, with 1700 as the base year. The Lancashire index is a simple series of price relatives, on a 1700 base, of the daily labor on buildings and roads'. Miss Gilboy concludes that 'Regional differences in the course of real wages in eighteenth century England are very evident'. Wages in London declined 'in the last half of the century. Real wages in the North, however, rose consistently. An index of real wages in the West of England would undoubtedly show a decline'.[34]

Cost of Living Index
1700=100

1700:	100	1724:	99	1748:	100	1772:	136	1796:	153
1701:	100	1725:	105	1749:	98	1773:	131	1797:	152
1702:	91	1726:	100	1750:	93	1774:	129	1798:	165
1703:	99	1727:	106	1751:	98	1775:	128	1799:	229
1704:	88	1728:	112	1752:	94	1776:	120	1800:	252
1705:	95	1729:	102	1753:	95	1777:	131	1801:	190
1706:	86	1730:	89	1754:	92	1778:	123	1802:	166
1707:	94	1731:	88	1755:	98	1779:	117	1803:	171
1708:	116	1732:	81	1756:	125	1780:	125	1804:	204
1709:	135	1733:	89	1757:	118	1781:	125	1805:	196
1710:	147	1734:	91	1758:	108	1782:	144	1806:	201
1711:	104	1735:	88	1759:	99	1783:	139	1807:	226
1712:	98	1736:	93	1760:	97	1784:	129	1808:	236
1713:	108	1737:	94	1761:	99	1785:	132	1809:	229
1714:	105	1738:	91	1762:	109	1786:	128	1810:	225
1715:	100	1739:	109	1763:	110	1787:	130	1811:	266
1716:	92	1740:	119	1764:	115	1788:	127	1812:	270
1717:	92	1741:	103	1765:	117	1789:	134	1813:	224
1718:	92	1742:	98	1766:	124	1790:	133	1814:	198
1719:	106	1743:	82	1767:	123	1791:	131	1815:	183
1720:	102	1744:	83	1768:	109	1792:	140		
1721:	91	1745:	94	1769:	108	1793:	148		
1722:	86	1746:	92	1770:	118	1794:	168		
1723:	97	1747:	95	1771:	130	1795:	179		

*Eden's work, see Note 29. David Davies, *The Case of the Laborers in Husbandry* (Bath 1795).

Wages index

1700 = 1000

Date	London		Lancs			Date	London		Lancs	
	1	2	1	2			1	2	1	2
1700	100	100	100	100		1749	118	120	133	136
1701	99	99	95	95		1750	120	129	133	143
1702	99	109	89	98		1751	118	120	133	136
1703	109	110	89	90		1752	118	126	133	141
1704	114	130	89	101		1753	118	124	133	140
1705	109	115	105	111		1754	118	128	133	145
1706	109	127	105	122		1755	118	120	133	136
1707	109	116	105	112		1756	118	94	133	106
1708	109	94	105	90		1757	118	100	111	94
1709	111	82	89	66		1758	118	109	111	103
1710	109	74	105	71		1759	118	119	133	134
1711	110	106	105	101		1760	118	122	123	123
1712	110	112	105	107		1761	118	119	123	124
1713	110	102	100	93		1762	118	108	123	113
1714	109	104	111	106		1763	121	110	177	161
1715	109	109	111	111		1764	121	105	156	136
1716	109	118	111	121		1765	121	103	156	133
1717	109	118	89	97		1766	121	98	156	126
1718	109	118	111	121		1767	121	98	156	127
1719	109	103	111	105		1768	121	111	200	183
1720	110	108	133	130		1769	121	112	200	185
1721	110	121	123	135		1770	121	103	200	169
1722	110	128	123	143		1771	121	93	177	136
1723	110	113	123	127		1772	121	89	200	147
1724	110	111	123	124		1773	121	92	200	153
1725	110	105	111	106		1774	121	94	200	155
1726	110	110	111	111		1775	118	92	200	156
1727	110	104	133	126		1776	118	98	200	167
1728	105	94	111	99		1777	118	90	200	153
1729	110	108	133	130		1778	118	96	200	163
1730	109	122	133	149		1779	123	105	200	171
1731	114	130	123	140		1780	123	98	200	160
1732	114	141	133	164		1781	123	98	200	160
1733	114	128	133	149		1782	123	85	211	147
1734	114	125	133	146		1783	123	88	200	144
1735	118	134	133	151		1784	123	95	189	146
1736	116	125	133	143		1785	123	93	205	155
1737	118	126	133	141		1786	123	96	223	174
1738	116	127	133	146		1787	123	95	211	162
1739	118	108	133	122		1788			228	180
1740	116	97	133	112		1789			228	170
1741	116	113	133	129		1790			233	175
1742	118	120	133	136		1791			223	170
1743	115	140	133	162		1792			200	143
1744	118	142	133	160		1793			267	180
1745	118	126	133	141		1794			233	133
1746	118	128	128	139		1795			233	130
1747	118	124	128	135		1796			233	152
1748	118	118	133	133						

Column 1 = money wages
Column 2 = real wages

(Gilboy pp.137 and 140, Mitchell pp.346-7)

Work in a fifteenth century Mint. In the centre a hammerman is beating out a sheet of silver to a uniform thickness. On his right large shears are used to cut out blanks from such a sheet. On his left the master craftsman is striking coins from blanks trimmed by his assistant standing at the bench. Behind these craftsmen the Master of the Mint checks his accounts. The balance used for assaying is beside him. In practice the various operations would have been carried out in separate workshops.

Mint Press Room at the Tower of London in the eighteenth century. Reproduced by permission of The Museum of London.

THE NINETEENTH CENTURY (1780-1914)

Many statistical studies of wages and the cost of living in the nineteenth century have been published since 1900. Information from some of these studies was reproduced in the first edition of this book. In three articles, published in 1990, 1991, and 1995,[35] Professor Charles Feinstein has brought together all this information, looked at it critically, and produced new, systematic indexes. It seemed simpler to give the working local historian the major, relevant results of Feinstein's work, rather than to reproduce again some of the older tables. Some of these are listed at the end of this book.

N. J. Silberling: Cost of Living.

Feinstein's new cost of living index for 1780-1870 is the successor to 'at least nine overall price indices which cover all or most of the period 1780-1850' (1995, p 9). One of these, N. J. Silberling's, was much used by historians; it led to a controversy which reveals some of the dangers which local and family historians must avoid.

Silberling compiled a cost-of-living index for this period which was statistically more sophisticated than its predecessors because he had much more numerical information available. His aim was 'to measure variations in the prices of various articles, having regard to their relative importance in, and effect upon, the provisioning and clothing of typical working-class families'. To calculate the 'relative weighting to be assigned to articles of food and fuel for such normal budgets', Silberling drew on three 'studies... for representative industrial areas at various intervals from 1790 on'. Some of these were for a later date and in general their source material was inadequate. Silberling claimed, rather boldly, that

> a high degree of uniformity was found in the results of different investigators and for different periods of time. It is a familiar statistical fact that the proportions of expenditure for food, clothing, etc., tend to be fairly constant for large masses of the common people.

Historians today would be less assured. Fifteen important commodities were included in Silberling's index. Their relative importance in the index was in the proportions: food and tobacco 42; clothing materials 8; fuel, etc., 6. This was the 'weighting'. These three major groupings were made up as follows:

Food and tobacco: wheat 15, mutton 6, beef 6, butter 5, oats 3, sugar 3, tea 2,
   coffee 1, tobacco 1.
Clothing materials: wool 3, cotton 3, flax 1, leather 1.
Fuel, etc: coal 4, tallow 2.

Silver halfpennies of Henry VIII issued in the reign
of Edward VI, 1547-51.

These were 'only raw materials, and the prices are those of the wholesale markets, which do not vary exactly with retail prices of finished products'. Silberling was modest enough to claim only 'that the indices profess to be no more than reasonably good approximations'.[36]

Unfortunately Silberling's index was widely and wrongly used, notably by Sir John Clapham, to argue that 'on the average the potential standard of comfort of an English rural labouring family in 1824 was probably a trifle better than it had been in 1794'.[37] Clapham, who was a very great economic historian, nevertheless made two statistical blunders. In working out his 'average' rural labourer's wage he did not allow for the different numbers of labourers in each county, but simply averaged the different county wages as though they were equally weighted. What he should have done is explained on p. 21. G. D. H. Cole pointed out that Silberling's index was in any case inappropriate as a measure of the rural labourer's standard of living:

> The index is based mainly on urban living conditions, and assigns an undue weight to commodities which the labourer could not afford to buy. The labourer lived mainly on cereals, even when he was not driven to subsist on potatoes; and accordingly he suffered terribly in the years of high cereal prices.[38]

Clapham had accepted that 'Prof. Silberling could not take account of potatoes'.[39]

Charles Feinstein: cost of living

Feinstein's critique of Silberling, and the other indexes for the period, pointed out that most of them were essentially wholesale or contract price indexes. Only Wood, in 1899, 'compiled an index of retail prices', and he argued 'that the use of wholesale price index numbers when calculating real wages is not justifiable', as they differed substantially from his retail price index. Feinstein commented: 'wholesale prices are clearly incorrect in principle'. He then investigated how far retail and wholesale prices actually diverged. 'For food and fuel [there was no] significant difference [but] for clothing a very different picture emerges' (1995, pp. 10-11). Changes in the price of cloth, used in the wholesale indexes, diverged greatly from the costs of garments.

Feinstein then considered the weightings given to the different objects included in these early indexes. 'The weights assigned to the broad categories of food, fuel (including light) and clothing show only modest differences, and there is [agreement about] rent. There is, however, markedly more variation in the food sub-weights'.

Allocation of working-class expenditure on food (%).

	Bread, flour, oatmeal (1)	Potatoes, beans etc (2)	Meat, fish (3)	Butter, cheese, milk (4)	Sugar, tea (5)
1. Phelps Brown and Hopkins	26	7	41	20	6
2. Davies and Eden, 1787-96	62	4	13	9	12
3. Ashton, 1791-1831	53	13	20	13	0
4. Silberling, 1790-1850	44	0	29	12	15
5. Wood, 1840	48	6	18	17	11
6. Lindert and Williamson, 1850	68	0	18	7	7
7. Mackenzie, 1860	58	13	11	9	9
8. Board of Trade, 1904	23	5	37	23	12

(1995. p. 19)

'It is immediately evident that bread and flour are given an appreciably larger weight in Lindert and Williamson's southern urban series than in any other budgets' (1995, pp. 19-20).

With all this in mind Feinstein constructed a new index covering 'food (11 categories), alcoholic drink, fuel and light, clothing and footwear, and rent'. He explains his 'choice of base years and the type of index number to be used', as well as his 'choice of weights'. These are explained in detail with a particular emphasis on the difficulty of calculating rent. This is invaluable reading for anyone concerned with changes in the standard of living during the nineteenth century (1995, pp. 20-21).

(top) **Silver testoon** (shilling) of Henry VIII, 1544-7.

(bottom) **Silver groat** of Edward VI, but in the name of Henry VIII, 1547-9.

Silver shilling of Elizabeth I, 1560-61.

New cost-of-living index.
1780-1870 (1820-24 = 100)

1780	68.4	1810	134.9	1840	105.0
1781	74.3	1811	136.6	1841	102.2
1782	73.8	1812	152.5	1842	98.2
1783	73.1	1813	149.5	1843	89.4
1784	71.4	1814	129.5	1844	92.6
1785	69.3	1815	107.2	1845	91.4
1786	67.9	1816	120.9	1846	103.7
1787	69.4	1817	127.2	1847	116.0
1788	71.8	1818	118.6	1848	97.3
1789	72.8	1819	113.5	1849	93.7
1790	76.1	1820	108.6	1850	88.2
1791	74.2	1821	101.4	1851	84.3
1792	72.8	1822	94.0	1852	85.7
1793	77.2	1823	95.8	1853	99.7
1794	80.1	1824	100.3	1854	108.3
1795	93.4	1825	105.5	1855	110.1
1796	98.1	1826	98.4	1856	109.9
1797	87.1	1827	96.6	1857	106.4
1798	87.8	1828	96.2	1858	95.3
1799	99.6	1829	100.7	1859	95.9
1800	131.3	1830	97.7	1860	103.7
1801	136.5	1831	98.8	1861	105.9
1802	102.8	1832	94.6	1862	105.6
1803	99.5	1833	91.5	1863	100.5
1804	106.5	1834	89.5	1864	98.9
1805	122.6	1835	84.7	1865	100.4
1806	114.8	1836	91.0	1866	107.1
1807	109.6	1837	96.4	1867	115.5
1808	116.4	1838	98.8	1868	111.3
1809	131.1	1839	106.0	1869	102.0
				1870	102.5

(1995. p. 26)

In his 1991 article Feinstein constructed a new cost of living index for 1870-1914 which differs substantially from 'the index published by Bowley in 1937, and generally used since' (1991, p, 174). The new index 'includes some items previously omitted from cost of living indexes for this period, notably drink and tobacco and some services, and is weighted on the basis of new estimates of the pattern of expenditure of working-class households in 1900' (1995, p. 28). The table shows the components, their weighting in the first line, and how this weighting changed in each year. As Feinstein pointed out: 'Our concern is with changes over time, not with levels' (1995, p. 10).

Cost of Living Index 1870-1914 (1900 = 100)

	Food	Rent and rates	Clothing	Fuel and light	Cleaning materials	Drink and tobacco	Furniture and other goods	Travel	Other services	TOTAL
	48.3	8.7	7.8	4.6	0.9	18.0	3.0	4.3	4.4	100.0
1870	125.3	71.6	129.5	104.1	145.5	97.3	92.0	126.2	100.0	113.1
1871	131.6	71.6	128.9	103.6	142.1	97.6	100.1	126.7	100.0	116.3
1872	138.3	72.2	135.7	118.5	147.2	97.8	109.3	127.2	100.0	121.2
1873	138.2	73.4	136.1	131.0	148.9	97.8	113.5	130.7	100.0	122.1
1874	129.4	74.2	132.5	112.8	145.5	97.9	107.4	130.0	100.0	116.6
1875	126.7	74.7	131.2	106.2	143.8	97.9	104.7	127.5	100.0	114.8
1876	128.2	76.1	124.5	110.4	149.3	97.9	102.3	123.1	100.0	115.1
1877	129.8	77.0	119.8	102.0	135.9	97.8	103.1	122.1	100.0	115.0
1878	124.1	77.8	116.8	92.3	135.9	98.1	99.1	119.9	100.0	111.5
1879	115.5	78.7	110.7	88.1	130.5	98.3	96.1	116.8	100.0	106.5
1880	120.5	79.5	111.3	80.1	135.9	98.4	98.7	114.9	100.0	108.7
1881	117.7	80.5	108.5	83.4	124.4	98.4	98.5	114.0	100.0	107.3
1882	118.7	81.1	107.5	77.5	129.9	98.5	99.5	114.6	100.0	107.5
1883	118.5	81.6	105.1	80.0	128.2	98.4	103.3	113.1	100.0	107.5
1884	111.4	82.3	102.7	79.4	128.1	98.4	102.6	113.0	100.0	103.8
1885	104.1	83.3	102.1	79.8	117.0	98.5	100.0	111.4	100.0	100.2
1886	102.9	84.1	102.2	78.1	103.6	98.5	98.8	109.0	100.0	99.3
1887	99.2	84.7	102.2	75.1	99.3	98.2	98.1	108.9	100.0	97.3
1888	98.8	85.3	100.8	76.5	96.5	97.9	99.1	108.7	100.0	97.1
1889	100.4	85.7	100.4	76.5	96.8	98.1	100.1	108.8	100.0	97.9
1890	100.2	86.0	101.8	81.3	95.4	98.5	100.7	109.2	100.0	98.3
1891	102.1	86.3	101.9	79.8	97.1	98.5	100.2	108.6	100.0	99.1
1892	102.8	87.2	101.0	79.4	101.2	98.5	99.9	107.8	100.0	99.5

1893	98.1	89.3	100.3	84.5	102.6	98.3	100.9	107.9	100.0	97.6
1894	94.0	91.1	99.1	74.4	97.9	98.4	98.5	105.5	100.0	95.0
1895	91.8	92.6	97.8	72.5	87.7	98.6	95.4	105.0	100.0	93.7
1896	90.9	93.8	98.6	74.3	89.4	99.0	96.0	103.3	100.0	93.5
1897	94.8	95.4	98.2	74.0	83.6	99.0	96.8	101.1	100.0	95.4
1898	98.3	97.1	97.0	73.8	82.5	98.8	97.3	100.8	100.0	97.1
1899	95.4	98.6	96.2	79.7	94.9	98.9	96.00	100.4	100.0	96.1
1900	100.0	100.0	100.0	100.0	100.0	100.0	100.0	100.0	100.0	100.0
1901	99.6	101.7	100.6	94.0	98.1	100.7	97.3	99.2	100.0	99.7
1902	99.8	103.8	99.9	89.3	99.8	100.6	98.2	98.6	100.0	99.7
1903	101.4	106.3	99.7	88.3	100.7	100.5	100.7	98.7	100.0	100.8
1904	100.4	107.7	102.3	86.3	101.5	100.5	97.7	98.5	100.0	100.4
1905	101.0	108.4	103.0	84.8	97.1	100.5	101.1	97.8	100.0	100.8
1906	100.5	108.9	104.5	85.8	100.7	100.9	100.5	96.8	100.0	100.7
1907	102.7	109.1	106.2	92.7	109.2	100.9	99.5	97.1	100.0	102.3
1908	104.9	109.8	107.1	90.7	107.8	101.2	102.6	97.1	100.0	103.6
1909	105.1	110.6	108.4	87.8	108.0	101.8	100.8	96.4	100.0	103.8
1910	107.2	111.9	110.7	84.8	112.0	107.3	102.4	96.7	100.0	106.0
1911	107.0	112.6	112.4	85.2	111.7	107.6	104.8	97.1	100.0	106.3
1912	111.9	113.5	115.5	88.3	110.0	107.7	106.1	100.0	100.0	109.3
1913	112.9	114.8	115.9	91.9	111.4	107.6	105.9	100.2	100.0	110.0
1914	114.8	115.0	117.4	89.4	117.2	117.5	107.0	100.7	100.0	112.8

(1991, pp.170-71)

Charles Feinstein: real earnings

To measure real earnings these two cost of living indexes were linked together and related to two of Feinstein's indexes of nominal wages. Such indexes try 'to measure the overall trends in nominal wages in the United Kingdom with full allowance for shifts in the composition of the labour force'. This is extremely difficult to achieve for the earlier period 'when factory employment displaced handworking and domestic activity in many sectors' (1995, p. 6). So Feinstein used an 'index of money wages linking the Wood/Bowley series for 1790-1830, [only using his own] provisional index for 1830-70' (1995, p. 29). This provisional index is 'limited to the major industries of agriculture, building, coal mining, engineering and shipbuilding, cotton, wool and worsted, iron-making and printing' (1995,p. 6). For the later period, 1880-1913, Feinstein used an 'index of average earnings.. built up from a series for 35 occupations or industries' (1995, p. 7), which he had published in 1990. The table which follows brings together these indexes, covering selected years, 'mainly those in which there were cyclical turning points in the index of real earnings' (1995, p. 29).

Silver halfpennies of Elizabeth I, 1595/6 and 1597/8.

(top) **Silver crown** of William and Mary, 1692.

(bottom) **Silver Maundy coins** — 4d., 3d., 2d., 1d. — of William and Mary, 1689 and 1691.

Indices of nominal earnings, cost of living
and real earnings, selected years, 1790-1990 (1913=100).

	Nominal earnings (1)	Cost of living (2)	Real earnings (3)
1790	29	76	38
1795	34	94	36
1800	39	132	29
1805	44	123	36
1810	49	135	36
1816	47	121	39
1820	43	109	40
1824	42	101	42
1830	40	98	40
1835	40	85	47
1840	43	105	41
1845	44	92	48
1851	45	85	53
1856	55	110	49
1861	55	106	52
1866	62	108	58
1873	75	111	67
1876	74	105	71
1881	71	98	73
1886	71	90	79
1891	78	90	86
1896	79	85	93
1901	87	91	96
1906	90	92	98
1913	100	100	100
1918	211	202	104
1920	278	245	114
1924	198	172	115
1929	197	162	122
1932	189	142	133
1936	197	145	136
1938	209	154	135
1948	456	270	169
1951	546	315	173
1955	729	377	194
1960	949	429	221
1968	1509	568	266
1973	2685	783	343
1979	6236	1946	320
1983	10091	2917	346
1990	17574	4329	406

(1995, p. 31)

The Times of Payment.

	£ S D
In May 1776 including the Money Dickenson has Received	300 - 0 - 0
In September	300 - 0 - 0
In January 1777	250 - 0 - 0
On finishing the Work	250 - 0 - 0
	£ 1100 - 0 - 0

Mr. Dickenson has rec.d of Mr. Burnet in part of the first payment 163gr 0s 0c

Lancelot Brown

Terms of payment for work at Sherborne Castle, signed by Lancelot ('Capability') Brown (1776-1777). Reproduced by permission of Sherborne Castle Estates.

A room at the Bank of England in about 1695 when the Bank was housed at Grocers' Hall, Poultry. The Bank did not move to Threadneedle Street until 1734. Reproduced by permission of the Governor and Company of the Bank of England.

TWENTIETH-CENTURY OFFICIAL
(GOVERNMENT) INDEXES

Cost of Living

The origin and purpose of the first official cost-of-living index, introduced in 1914, was explained in a government publication:

> The official cost-of-living index figures were instituted in the early states of the war of 1914-18 with a view to measuring the percentage increase month by month in the cost of maintaining unchanged the standard of living prevailing among working-class households in July, 1914 ... The index is designed to measure the average percentage changes in the retail prices of a fixed list of commodities and services bought by working-class households. It does not purport to reflect changes in expenditure resulting from alterations in supplies or consumption.[40]

It was based on sample budgets of working-class spending, collected in 1904. The cost of buying, in 1914, the items in the average, standard family budget of 1904 was calculated, and these 1914 costs were used to provide the statistics for the 'base year'. It was not altogether a coincidence that what evidence we have suggests that in the year 1904 the working-class standard of living, what current money wages would buy, was at its lowest level for over ten years, and that, by 1914, it was some three per cent higher than in 1904. So the exceptionally low living standard of 1904 was used as the statistical measure of change. This index was used until 1947! The Interim Index of Retail Prices introduced in June 1947 was based on a new set of family budgets collected in 1937-8, and given a weighting as of 17 June 1947.

The changes made in later indexes were explained in successive editions of the *Annual Abstract of Statistics*, as follows:

> From February 1952 certain changes were made in the method of calculating the index. In particular, a new set of weights was introduced based on estimates of consumption in 1950, valued at 15 January 1952 prices.

This still covered the expenditure of working-class families only. This 'Interim Index of Retail Prices was discontinued after January 1956, and was replaced by a new index',[41] which was 'based on ascertained consumption in 1953-4, valued at 17 January 1956 prices'.[42]

> Commencing in January 1962 the weights have been revised each January on the bases of ascertained consumption in the three years ended in the previous June, valued at prices obtaining at the date of revision.[43]

The *Annual Abstracts* have a full explanation of current practice:

> The retail prices index measures the change from month to month in the average level of prices of goods and services purchased by most households in the United Kingdom. The expenditure pattern on which the index is based is revised each year using information from the Family Expenditure Survey. The expenditure of certain higher income households and households of retired people dependent mainly on social security benefits is excluded.

> The index covers a large and representative selection of more than 600 separate goods and services ... measured in more than 180 towns ... Approximately 150,000 separate price quotations are used in compiling the index.

This is the 1995 version. In 1987 it was '130,000 separate price quotations', in 1991 only 120,000. From 1975 'the weights have been revised on expenditure for the latest available year'.[44]

Weighting

The weighting used in compiling these indexes was as follows:

	Jul 1914	17 Jun 1947	Feb 1952	1962	1970	1980	1985	1990		1990	1991	1994
Food	60	348	399	319	255	214	190	158	}	205	198	187
Catering	–							47	}			
Meals bought & consumed outside house	–				43	41	45					
Alcoholic drink	–	} 217	78	64	66	82	75	77	}	111	109	111
Tobacco	–		90	79	64	40	37	34	}			
Housing	–	–	–	102	119	124	153	185	}			
Durable household goods	–	71	62	64	60	69	65	71				
Household services								40	}	346	353	326
Fuel & light	8	65	66	62	61	59	65	50				
Rent & rates	16	88	72	–	–	–	–	–	}			
Clothing & footwear	12	97	98	98	86	84	75	69	}			
Miscellaneous goods	4	35	44	64	65	74	77	–		108	101	95
Services	–	79	91	56	55	62	62					
Personal services	–	–	–	–	–	–	–	39	}			
Transport & vehicles	–	–	–	92	126	151	156					
Motoring expenses								131	}			
Fares & other travel expenses								21				
Leisure goods								48	}	230	239	281
Leisure services								30	}			
TOTAL	100	1000	1000	1000	1000	1000	1000	1000		1000	1000	1000

(top) **Copper halfpenny of George I, 1717.**

(bottom) **Copper halfpenny of George II, 1742.**

Indexes of retail prices.

The various index and weighting figures follow:

Year	July 1914=100	1 Sept. 1939=100
1914	100	
1915	123	
1916	146	
1917	176	
1918	203	
1919	215	
1920	249	
1921	226	
1922	183	
1923	174	
1924	175	
1925	176	
1926	172	
1927	167.5	
1928	166	
1929	164	
1930	158	
1931	147.5	
1932	144	
1933	140	
1934	141	
1935	143	
1936	147	
1937	154	
1938	156	101
1939	158	102
1940	184	119
1941	199	128
1942	200	129
1943	199	128
1944	201	130
1945	203	131
1946	203.5	131
1947(June)	203	131 = 100 (17 June)

Year	17 June 1947=100	15 Jan. 1952=100
1948	108	
1949	111	
1950	114	
1951	125	
1952	136	102.6
1953	140	105.8
1954	143	107.7
1955	149	112.6
1956	153.4	115.8

	17 Jan. 1956=100	16 Jan. 1962 = 100
1956	102.0	
1957	105.8	
1958	109.0	
1959	109.6	
1960	110.7	
1961	114.5	
1962	117.5	101.6
1963		103.6
1964		107.0
1965		112.1
1966		116.5
1967		119.4
1968		125.0
1969		131.8
1970		140.2
1971		153.4
1972		164.3
1973		179.4
1974		208.2

100 = 15 Jan. 1974: 191.8

Year	15 Jan 1974 = 100	Year	15 Jan 1974 = 100	Year	15 Jan 1987 = 100
1974	108.5	1981	295.0	1987	101.9
1975	134.8	1982	320.4	1988	106.9
1976	157.1	1983	335.1	1989	115.2
1977	182.0	1984	351.8	1990	126.1
1978	197.1	1985	373.2	1991	133.5
1979	223.5	1986	385.9	1992	138.57
1980	263.7			1993	140.7
				1994	144.1

(The statistics are taken from the *Statistical Abstracts for the U.K.: 1910-24, 1913* and *1924-37*, and from the *Annual Abstract of Statistics* for 1938-49, no. 87, p. 281; 1956, no. 93, p.292; 1960, no. 97, p. 296; 1970, no. 107, p. 363; 1987, no. 123, p. 320; 1988, no. 124, p. 317; 1991, No. 127, p. 328; 1995, No. 131, p. 336).

These indexes have been combined with others into a single index of retail prices, covering the years from 1900. It is based on the following: for 1900-14, an index based on working-class expenditure on food and coal, for London only, and clothing; for 1914-38, the official cost-of-living index of essentials, weighted by working-class expenditure in 1914 (pp.55-57 *above*); for 1938-January 1952, interpolation of estimated figures for 1938, June 1947, and January 1952; and from 1952 January, the successive indexes printed above.

Copper penny of George III, 1806.

Index of retail prices 1900-1992

Year		Year		Year		Year	
1900 :	19	1923 :	37	1946 :	51	1969 :	127
1901 :	19	1924 :	37	1947 :	54	1970 :	135
1902 :	19	1925 :	37	1948 :	57	1971 :	148
1903 :	19	1926 :	36	1949 :	59	1972 :	159
1904 :	19	1927 :	35	1950 :	61	1973 :	173
1905 :	19	1928 :	35	1951 :	67	1974 :	201
1906 :	19	1929 :	35	1952 :	73	1975 :	250
1907 :	20	1930 :	33	1953 :	75	1976 :	291
1908 :	20	1931 :	31	1954 :	76	1977 :	337
1909 :	20	1932 :	30	1955 :	80	1978 :	365
1910 :	20	1933 :	30	1956 :	84	1979 :	414
1911 :	21	1934 :	30	1957 :	87	1980 :	488
1912 :	21	1935 :	30	1958 :	90	1981 :	546
1913 :	21	1936 :	31	1959 :	90	1982 :	593
1914 :	21	1937 :	32	1960 :	91	1983 :	620
1915 :	26	1938 :	33	1961 :	94	1984 :	651
1916 :	30	1939 :	34	1962 :	98	1985 :	691
1917 :	37	1940 :	38	1963 :	100	1986 :	714
1918 :	42	1941 :	42	1964 :	103	1987 :	744
1919 :	46	1942 :	45	1965 :	108	1988 :	781
1920 :	52	1943 :	47	1966 :	112	1989 :	841
1921 :	47	1944 :	47	1967 :	115	1990 :	921
1922 :	38	1945 :	49	1968 :	121	1991 :	975
						1992 :	1015

(*The British Economy: Key Statistics 1900-74* and *Annual Abstract of Statistics,* quoted in D. and G. Butler, *British Political Facts 1900-94* (1994), pp. 383-4)

Purchasing power of the pound, 1900-1993.

Year		Year		Year		Year	
1900 :	35.87	1924 :	17.65	1948 :	15.32	1972 :	5.55
1901 :	35.58	1925 :	17.38	1949 :	14.17	1973 :	5.17
1902 :	35.02	1926 :	17.76	1950 :	13.70	1974 :	4.65
1903 :	34.75	1927 :	17.76	1951 :	13.19	1975 :	3.95
1904 :	34.48	1928 :	18.59	1952 :	11.70	1976 :	3.23
1905 :	34.75	1929 :	18.67	1953 :	11.22	1977 :	2.81
1906 :	36.76	1930 :	18.82	1954 :	11.08	1978 :	2.58
1907 :	33.70	1931 :	20.36	1955 :	10.65	1979 :	2.38
1908 :	32.95	1932 :	21.22	1956 :	10.13	1980 :	2.06
1909 :	32.95	1933 :	21.95	1957 :	9.73	1981 :	1.85
1910 :	32.71	1934 :	21.95	1958 :	9.39	1982 :	1.68
1911 :	32.23	1935 :	21.74	1959 :	9.21	1983 :	1.61
1912 :	31.11	1936 :	21.25	1960 :	9.24	1984 :	1.55
1913 :	31.11	1937 :	20.64	1961 :	9.06	1985 :	1.49
1914 :	31.33	1938 :	19.65	1962 :	8.67	1986 :	1.42
1915 :	27.64	1939 :	20.08	1963 :	8.45	1987 :	1.38
1916 :	23.07	1940 :	17.93	1964 :	8.29	1988 :	1.34
1917 :	18.90	1941 :	15.97	1965 :	7.94	1989 :	1.27
1918 :	16.67	1942 :	15.63	1966 :	7.62	1990 :	1.18
1919 :	14.26	1943 :	15.69	1967 :	7.36	1991 :	1.08
1920 :	13.91	1944 :	15.69	1968 :	7.18	1992 :	1.02
1921 :	11.89	1945 :	15.47	1969 :	6.78	1993 :	1.00
1922 :	16.25	1946 :	15.42	1970 :	6.47		
1923 :	17.51	1947 :	15.32	1971 :	5.99		

Bank of England Retail Price Index.

Wage Rates

The published official tables are confusing because of changes, gaps and overlaps. From 1920 to 1935 a table of the 'estimated average percentage increase in weekly full-time rates of wages generally compared with July 1914' was published. The index stopped in August 1935. With an index figure of July 1914 = 100 the table reads:

31 December			
1920 :	270/280	1928 :	170/175
1921 :	210/215	1929 :	170/174
1922 :	170/175	1930 :	170/174
1923 :	165/170	1931 :	166/170
1924 :	170/175	1932 :	165
1925 :	175	1933 :	164
1926 :	175	1934 :	165
1927 :	170/175	1935 :	168

(*Statistical Abstracts for the U.K.*: 1911-25, 1912-26, 1913-32, 1913 and 1922-35, 1913 and 1923-36.)

These figures can be combined with those of the cost-of-living index for the same period to produce an index of real wages, as explained on p. 26. A new index of weekly wage rates with 1 September 1939 = 100 was published for the years 1935 to 1947; the figures represent the monthly range from January to December in each year. No annual averages were published.

1935 :	91/92	1942 :	127/133
1936 :	93/95	1943 :	133/139
1937 :	95/99	1944 :	139/146
1938 :	98/100	1945 :	145/153
1939 :	99/104	1946 :	157/165
1940 :	105/116	1947 :	165/173
1941 :	118/127		

(*Annual Abstract of Statistics*, 1935-46, no. 84 p. 118.)

The next index of weekly wage rates took 30 June 1947 = 100 as its base year. 'It is estimated that at the end of June 1947 the level of weekly full-time wage rates was between 166 and 167, taking September 1939 as 100'. So the 1939 and 1947 indexes can be related, taking 166/167 = 100. The new index, and those that followed up to 1977, distinguished the wage-rates of men, women, and juveniles, and had an all-in column. Below, we have omitted the column for juveniles.

30 June 1947 = 100

Year	All	Men	Women
1948	105.8	105.3	107.2
1949	108.6	108.0	110.8
1950	110.7	109.9	113.7
1951	120.0	119.0	123.4
1952	129.9	128.7	133.1
1953	136.0	134.4	140.3
1954	141.9	140.3	146.1
1955	151.4	150.0	154.7
1956 (Jan.)	156.0	154.0	160.0

(*Annual Abstract of Statistics*, 1958, no. 95, p. 127.)

31 January 1956 = 100 was the base year for the 'new series', which can 'be linked with the old series on a broad basis, by multiplying the new index figures by the following factors': All: 1.561 Men: 1.545 Women: 1.598. This series covered 'all industries and Services'.

Year & Month		All	Men	Women
1956	June	105.4	105.5	104.6
	December	106.4	106.3	106.3
1957	June	110.7	110.8	110.0
	December	112.2	112.1	112.1
1958	June	113.4	113.3	113.6
	December	116.2	116.2	116.0
1959	June	116.8	116.7	116.7
	December	117.5	117.3	118.0
1960	June	119.9	119.6	120.7
	December	122.3	121.9	122.7
1961	June	125.0	124.6	125.7
	December	126.4	126.0	126.5
1962	June	129.3	128.7	130.2
	December	132.0	131.3	133.3
1963	June	134.1	133.5	135.5
	December	137.7	137.0	139.3
1964	June	140.7	139.9	142.8
	December	143.0	142.1	145.3
1965	June	146.3	145.5	148.2
	December	149.6	148.3	153.6
1966	June	153.7	152.4	157.1
	December	154.6	153.2	158.7
1967	June	157.6	156.0	162.1
	December	163.7	162.4	167.3
1968	June	168.8	167.4	172.3
	December	175.4	174.3	177.7
1969	June	177.6	176.4	179.8
	December	185.5	184.4	184.6
1970	June	195.0	193.3	196.1
	December	210.6	208.5	212.5
1971	June	221.0	218.5	224.3
	December	236.6	233.2	242.5
1972	June	248.2	244.1	256.7
	July	249.5	245.2	259.0

(*Annual Abstract of Statistics*, 1965, no. 102, p. 131; 1970, no. 107, p. 149; 1976, no. 113, p. 170.)

Copper 'Cartwheel' twopence of George III, 1797.

31 July 1972 = 100

Year & Month		All	Men	Women
1972	December	108.1	108.3	106.9
1973	June	115.3	115.0	115.5
	December	121.4	120.9	123.7
1974	June	136.2	134.8	141.8
	December	157.1	153.9	170.9
1975	June	181.5	178.9	190.8
	December	197.0	192.1	219.0
1976	June	215.3	209.8	238.2
	December	220.2	213.3	250.6
1977	June	227.4		
	December	232.9		
1978	June	263.5		
	December	275.1		
1979	June	296.2		
	December	323.4		
1980	June	355.5		
	December	371.4		
1981	June	387.2		
	December	398.8		
1982	June	416.1		
	December	425.0		
1983	June	437.9		

'Separate indices for men, women and juveniles ceased to be published from January 1977'

(*Annual Abstract of Statistics*, 1980, no. 116, p. 167; 1984, no. 120, p. 125)

Calculation of these indices was discontinued after December 1983. From this date we must use statistics of earnings.

(c) *Deductions for Power, Standing-Room, Materials, &c.*—The chief illustration under this head lies in the circumstances of the case for which proceedings were taken (see above).   Miss Lennard found in Norfolk and Suffolk a considerable number and variety of deductions under this head similar to those reported in previous Annual Reports, especially in the industries of horsehair and silk-weaving, and in wholesale clothing, and she had to give many instructions as to technical failures to comply with the Act.

Miss Lennard.—The existence in the weaving trades of Norfolk and Suffolk of the custom of charging for the use of the work-room or hire of looms, especially where hand-looms are still solely or principally in use, has already been commented upon.   In addition, I have found in these districts several instances in which the hands were compelled to provide their own coal for fire or stove, and their own oil for lamps. The existence and nature of these charges seems to show that in this neighbourhood, where power has not yet succeeded in ousting completely the hand-loom, the industry has failed, so far, to emancipate itself entirely from the older domestic, and to develop into the modern factory, system. In the transition process there is, I think, in this trade some danger lest the revision of the piecework rates, which must necessarily accompany it, should lead temporarily to a low standard of wages, based as they are liable to be on the older nominal net earnings, without consideration of the decrease in real wages, which such prices represent.   With respect to all these deductions from wages, I have been struck by the apparent failure of both employer and employee to estimate the true net wage to which these charges reduce the gross.   Workers rarely are able to tell one how much out of the weekly wage goes to pay for materials used on an average, and the attempts of employer and employee to estimate this show sometimes considerable discrepancy.

Difficulties in calculating real earnings. From *The Annual Report of the Chief Inspector of Factories and Workshops*, 1913, Cd 7491 (1914), p. 109.

Earnings

The money figures for earnings in different employments were published for many years, but the first published 'monthly index of average earnings' seems to have been issued in 1970, with January 1970 = 100, but calculated backwards to 1967. Two sets of figures were published, before and after adjustments for seasonal variations. There are later indexes for the 'whole economy' with moveable base years. The first was calculated with January 1976 = 100; the second with January 1980 = 100. In the years 1976 to 1980 the first two indexes overlapped; for 1980 to 1982 the last two overlapped; for 1980 there are figures for all three indexes.

Date	Jan 1970 = 100 Unad	Adj	Jan 1976 = 100 Unad	Adj	Jan 1980 = 100 Both same	Jan 1985 = 100 Unad	Adj	Jan 1988 = 100 Both same	Jan 1990 = 100 Unad	Adj
1967	82.1	81.8								
1968	88.8	88.2								
1969	95.7	95.2								
1970	107.2	106.7								
1971	119.4	118.7								
1972	134.8	134.1								
1973	152.6	152.1								
1974	179.6	179.1								
1975	227.6	226.1								
1976	263.3	261.8	106.0	106.1						
1977	290.0	288.4	115.6	115.6						
1978	331.9	330.2	130.6	130.6						
1979	383.7	381.7	150.9	150.8						
1980	455.8	453.4	182.1	182.1	111.4					
1981			205.5	205.6	125.8					
1982			224.7	224.8	137.6	80.2	80.2			
1983					149.2	87.0	86.9			
1984					158.3	92.2	92.2			
1985					171.7	100.0	100.0			
1986					185.3	107.9	107.9			
1987					199.8	116.3	116.2			
1988						126.4	126.4	100	83.4	83.6
1989								109.1	91.2	91.2
1990								119.7	100.0	100.0
1991									108.0	107.5
1992									114.6	114.6
1993									118.5	118.5

(*Annual Abstract of Statistics*, 1982, no. 118, p. 175; 1984, no. 120, p. 128; 1987, no. 123, p. 126; 1989, no. 125, p. 123; 1991, no. 127, p. 125; 1992, no. 128, p. 125; 1995, no. 131, p. 118.)

NOTES

1. G. Baskerville, *English Monks and the Suppression of the Monasteries* (1937), pp.296-7

2. W. G. Hoskins, *The Age of Plunder* (1976), p.139n

3. *42nd Regional Cost of Living Report* (Sept 1987)

4. J. H. Clapham, *An Economic History of Modern Britain: Free Trade and Steel* (1932), p.285

5. M. J. Moroney, *Facts from Figures* (1951), pp.48-9

6. J. E. Thorold Rogers, *A History of Agriculture and Prices in England from 1259 to 1793* (7 vols., 1866-1900); W. H. Beveridge, *Prices and Wages in England from the Twelfth to the Nineteenth Century* (vol.1, 1939)

7. The numbers used in the examples in this section are the simplest, and bear no relation to real wages or prices.

8. Ministry of Labour, *The Cost of Living Index Number* (H.M.S.O. 1944), pp.3-4

9. Moroney, *Facts from Figures*, p.54

10. D. Seers, 'The increase in the working-class cost-of-living since before the war', in *Bulletin of the Oxford University Institute of Statistics*, vol.10 no.5 (May 1948), p.143

11. Moroney, *Facts from Figures*, pp.48-9, 50-2

12. See Table 1, 'The working-class share in pre-war consumption', in D. Seers, *Changes in the Cost-of-Living and the Distribution of Incomes since 1938* (1949), pp.26-7

13. D. Seers, *The Levelling of Incomes since 1938* (Oxford Institute of Statistics/Basil Blackwell, no date), p.21

14. Reported in *The Times*, 29 July 1977

15. *Social Trends* (1995 edition), pp.86 and 103-4

16. Index numbers are from a table on p.345 of B. R. Mitchell, *Abstract of British Historical Statistics* (1962), which is taken from E. C. Ramsbottom, 'The Course of Wage Rates in the U.K. 1921-34', in *Journal of the Royal Statistical Society* (1935). A. L. Bowley, *Wages and Income in the U.K. since 1860* (1937), p.30, has a similar table calculated with a different base year. On this page he explains how real wages are calculated but with a confusing misprint in the top line where 'column 2 by column 3' should clearly read 'column 1 by column 2'

17. *Statistical Abstract for the U.K. 1913 and 1919 to 1932* (H.M.S.O. 1934, Cmd.4489), pp.122-3

18. *Annual Abstract of Statistics* (1988), no.124, p.121 n.2

19. B. Seebohm Rowntree, *Poverty: a Study of Town Life* (1901) pp.29-30

20. B. Seebohm Rowntree, *Poverty and Progress* (1941), pp.26-7

21. L. M. Munby (ed.), *Early Stuart Household Accounts*, Hertfordshire Record Society (1986) pp.197-8 and x-xi

22. W. J. Hardy (ed.), *Hertford County Records: notes and extracts from the Sessions Rolls 1581-1698* (vol.1, 1905), pp.2, 8-12, 18, 35 and 292; W. le Hardy (ed.), *Calendar to the Sessions Books 1658-1700* (vol.6, 1930), pp.400-8. 442, 448, 460, 470, 476, 486 and 493-4; ibid., (vol.7, 1931), pp.3, 14, 26, 36, 48, 58, 68 and 85; A. E. Gibbs, *The Corporation Records of St Albans* (1890), pp.280-2

23. A. Palmer (ed.), *Tudor Churchwardens' Accounts*, Hertfordshire Record Society (1985), p.83

24. Munby, *Household Accounts*, pp.xxi-xxii

25. Palmer, *Churchwardens' Accounts*, pp.145-6, 152-4

26. Munby, *Household Accounts*, p.xxv

27. *Ibid.*, pp.xx and 63-8

28. Gibbs, *Corporation Records*, pp.281-2

29. Sir F. M. Eden, *The State of the Poor* (originally pub. 1797, abridged edition by A. G. L. Rogers, 1928), pp.135-6 and 337; Eden gives the expenditure of each family on rent, fuel, clothes etc. and suggests that the obvious gap between the Berkshire family's income and expenditure was made up from the local Poor Rates. There must be an error in Eden's table of the Berkshire family's expenditure: a shilling is presumably missing from the price of bacon, which should be 1s. 3d. per lb.

30. 'Seven centuries of the prices of consumables', in *Economica* (1955) [reprinted in E. M. Carus Wilson (ed.), *Essays in Economic History* (vol.2, 1962), pp.179-80, 182 and 188]

31. E. H. Phelps Brown and S. V. Hopkins, 'Wage-rates and prices', in *Economica*, vol.24 (1957), p.296

32. P. Bowden, 'Notes on statistical sources and methods', appendix to J. Thirsk (ed.), *The Agrarian History of England and Wales, IV, 1500-1640* (1967), pp.868-70; see also the Note on pp.865-70 of same volume, and Bowden's chapter 9, pp.593-695

33. P. Bowden, 'Statistics', in appendix 3 of J. Thirsk (ed.), *The Agrarian History of England and Wales, V, 1640-1750, II: Agrarian Change* (1985), pp.889-90, 892; see also the Note on pp.889-94 of the same volume, and Bowden's chapter 13, pp.1-118

34. B. R. Mitchell and P. Deane, *Abstract of British Historical Statistics* (1962), p.346 [editorial comment], and E. W. Gilboy, 'The Cost of Living and Real Wages in Eighteenth Century England', in *Review of Economic Statistics* vol.18 No.3 (Aug. 1936), pp.135, 138, 141

35. C. Feinstein, 'New estimates of average earnings in the United Kingdom, 1880-1913', in *Economic History Review* vol.43 (1990); C. Feinstein, 'A new look at the cost of living 1870-1914', in J. Foreman-Peck (ed.), *New Perspectives on the Late Victorian Economy* (1991); C. Feinstein, 'Changes in nominal wages, the cost of living and real wages in the United Kingdom over two centuries, 1780-1990', in E. Elgar (ed.), *Labour's Reward: Real Wages and Economic Change* (1995). Quotations from these works are referred to in the text by the year of the publication and the page number.

36. N. J. Silberling, 'British Prices and Business Cycles, 1779-1850', in supplement to the *Review of Economic Statistics* (1923), pp.234-5

37. Sir J. Clapham, *An Economic History of Modern Britain* (vol.1, 1939), pp.131 and 127n; for his argument see pp.vii and 127-31

38. G. D. H. Cole and R. Postgate, *The Common People 1746-1946* (1961-4 edition), p.204

39. Clapham, *Economic History*, p.127 n5

40. *The Cost of Living Index Number* (H.M.S.O., 1944), pp.1-2

41. *Annual Abstract of Statistics* (1956), no.93, p.292

42. *Ibid.* (1960), no.97, p.296

43. *Ibid.* (1979), no.107, p.363

44. *Ibid.* (1987), no.123, p.307-8; 1991, no. 127, p.309; 1995, no. 131, p.336.

Note on other sources

Apart from the many publications quoted in the text, few publications deal specifically with the problems met in calculating the changing value of money in the past.

In 1950 the Historical Association published E. Victor Morgan's *The Study of Prices and the Value of Money* in its 'Helps for Students' series. John Burnett's *A History of the Cost of Living* (Penguin, 1969) is a comprehensive study. Sidney Pollard and David W. Crossley include an invaluable 'Select Bibliography' in their book *The Wealth of Britain 1085-1966* (Batsford, 1968). Oksana Newman and Allan Foster, *The Value of a Pound: prices and incomes in Britain 1900-1993* (Gale Research International, 1995) contains very many details of money earnings in particular employments and prices of particular goods, with regional differences.

Below are some of the more important early attempts to measure the cost of living and earnings in the nineteenth century:

* G. H. Wood and A. L. Bowley, articles in the *Journal of the Royal Statistical Society* between 1898 and 1910, and in the *Economic Journal* for 1898 and 1899.

* T. S. Ashton, article in *The Manchester School* (1948); this and one of Wood's articles were reprinted in E. M. Carus Wilson (ed.), *Essays in Economic History* (vol.3, 1962), pp.132 et seq. and 237 et seq.

* B. R. Mitchell and P. Deane, in *Abstract of British Historical Statistics* (1962), made use of this work to construct their own indexes, pp.343-5

* A. L. Bowley, *Wages and Income in the United Kingdom since 1860* (1937) is a more up-to-date version of his earlier work.

* C. Feinstein, in his 1995 article (see note 35, above) mentions many later studies.